# MISSIOLOGY
*and the*
Social
Sciences

OTHER TITLES IN EMS SERIES

#1 SCRIPTURE AND STRATEGY: The Use of the Bible in Postmodern Church and Mission, by David J. Hesselgrave

#2 CHRISTIANITY AND THE RELIGIONS: A Biblical Theology of World Religions, Edward Rommen and Harold Netland, Editors

#3 SPIRITUAL POWER AND MISSIONS: Raising the Issues, Edward Rommen, Editor

# MISSIOLOGY
## *and the* Social Sciences
### Contributions, Cautions and Conclusions

Edward Rommen and Gary Corwin
Editors

**Evangelical Missiological Society Series #4**

visit us at missionbooks.org

*Missiology and the Social Sciences: Contributions, Cautions, and Conclusions*

Copyright 1996 by Evangelical Missiological Society
All Rights Reserved

No part of this book may be reproduced, stored in a retrieval system, or transmitted in any form or by any means—electronic, mechanical, photocopy, recording, or otherwise—without prior written permission from the publisher, except brief quotations used in connection with reviews in magazines or newspapers. For permission, email permissions@wclbooks.com. For corrections, email editor@wclbooks.com.

Published by William Carey Publishing (formerly William Carey Library)
10 W. Dry Creek Cir
Littleton, CO 80120 | www.missionbooks.org

William Carey Publishing is a ministry of Frontier Ventures
Pasadena, CA | www.frontierventures.org

ISBN: 978-1-64508-517-1 (paperback)

Printed Worldwide
27 26 25 24 23   2 3 4 5 6   IN

Library of Congress data on file with the publisher.

# CONTENTS

**PREFACE**
  David J. Hesselgrave                                              1

**PART I  MISSIOLOGY AND THE SOCIAL SCIENCES**

1. Introduction: An Appeal for Balance                              7
   *Michael Pocock*
2. Sociology and Missiology: Reflections on Mission Research       19
   *Gary R. Corwin*
3. The Contribution of Cultural Anthropology to Missiology         30
   *Norman E. Allison*
4. Prototype Semantics: Insights for Intercultural Communication   47
   *K. A. McElhanon*
5. Pychology and Missions: A History of Member Care in
   Cross-Cultural Ministry                                         75
   *Brent Lindquist*
6. The Contribution Of Technology To Missiology                    84
   *Ron Rowland*
7. Economics and Mission                                          102
   *Andreas J. Köstenberger*

**PART II  USE AND MISUSE OF THE SOCIAL SCIENCES**

8. A Critique of Charles Kraft's Use/Misuse of Communication &
   Social Sciences in Biblical Interpretation & Missiological
   Formulation                                                    121
   *Enoch Wan*
9. Use and Misuse of the Social Sciences: Interpreting the Biblical
   Text                                                           165
   *Robertson McQuilkin*
10. The Social Sciences and Missions: Applying the Message        184
    *Paul G. Hiebert*

**PART III  CONCLUSIONS**

11. Conclusions                                                   217
    *Edward Rommen*

# PREFACE

## David J. Hesselgrave[1]

The missiological enterprise is rooted in three types of source materials—God's revelation in Holy Scripture and the church creeds and theological systems based on that revelation; the social and behavioral sciences that help us understand the world's peoples and their cultures, belief systems and customs; and past and present missionary experience with its successes and failures. To explore any missiological issue without seeking out and examining relevant data from all three of these repositories of information is to truncate missiological inquiry and place both missionary theory and practice in jeopardy.

Moreover, since the mission with which we are concerned and in which we are involved is first and foremost God's mission and not our own, in all our missiological deliberations priority must be given to God's special revelation in the Bible. There is no denying the fact that over the last century and more—and especially during the last half of the twentieth century—missions have benefitted greatly by involvement in, and interaction with, research in such areas as linguistics, anthropology, sociology, communication, comparative religions, and psychology. And there is no denying the fact that the study of missions history, missionary biography, church growth and the like has yielded insights that have served to steady the course of contemporary missionary endeavor and helped set the agenda for missions in the future.

At the same time, when we define missiology as the "science of mission," we *must* remember that "science" in this case is being used in the more classical sense of that body of knowledge related to the understanding and carrying out of our missionary task in the world. Though much information that results from human experience and reflection is valuable in

---

[1] Chairman, Publications Committee.

missionary endeavor, *only to the degree that the decisive and determinative desideratum of missionary knowledge emanates from, or conforms to, the Divine Word as we have it in Christ and Scripture can the "science of Mission" be truly Christian.*

That brings us to the significance of the present volume. Almost a decade ago in doing a thematic content analysis of the major articles appearing in the *International Review of Missions* and the *Evangelical Missions Quarterly* between 1973 and 1986 I discovered something rather surprising. Out of 949 articles in the *IRM*, a total of 145 articles were focused on theological themes, 34 on missions history, and only 14 on the contributions of the social sciences. In the *EMQ* the emphasis was very different. Out of 604 articles a total of 8 were focused on missions history, 45 on theological themes, and 38 on the contributions of the sciences (*Today's Choices for Tomorrow's Mission*, Zondervan: 1988, pp. 141-42). It goes beyond our present purpose to attempt an explanation for this rather astounding difference in the rootage of missions/missiology as reflected in these two periodicals, but it is important that we take note of the relatively heightened dependence upon social science concerns on the part of evangelical editors and writers. An acquaintance with the subject matter of evangelical literature on the missionary enterprise that has appeared over the last forty or fifty years supports the conclusion that this interest borders on fascination.

As one whose writings have drawn rather extensively from these sciences, I am not inclined to disavow the fact that much of what has been learned about the world's peoples—to say nothing about that which has been borrowed from modern technology—is of great significance to missions. One is not well-advised to bite the hand that feeds us. On the other hand, one is well-advised to examine the food itself and decide whether or not it is wholesome, and in what proportions.

It is justifiable then, to review some of the ways in which the social sciences contribute to the missionary enterprise. It is also justifiable—no, it is incumbent upon us—to raise questions concerning matters of balance and priority. The present volume does both of these things. And because it does them so insightfully, lucidly and masterfully, we owe a special debt of gratitude to the editor, Edward Rommen, and the various contributors. And because the subject matter is so timely we commend this volume to the careful reading and serious study of every student of the Christian mission.

# PART I

# MISSIOLOGY AND THE SOCIAL SCIENCES

# 1

# INTRODUCTION: AN APPEAL FOR BALANCE

## Michael Pocock[1]

The principle reason for the existence of any professional society is to serve as a forum for the exchange of ideas among its members. This is true of the Evangelical Missiological Society (EMS), even though its constituency is intentionally broader than professional missiologists. The EMS seeks to unite in dialogue all who wish to think seriously about evangelical missiological concerns, whether they are pastors, field missionaries, mission executives, or researchers and professors of missions.[2] We all need to interact because we are inextricably bound together in the great enterprise of world evangelization and the missionary endeavor designed to achieve it. This paper is a call to enter our dialogue about missiology and the social sciences with objectivity, balance, and grace.

We shall look at the relationship between the social sciences and missiology. Presenters with a particular expertise in the various branches of the social sciences will address the society, explaining the scope and limitations of their discipline in informing the science of missiology. This is a good time to explore the theme because, as we shall see, among the thinkers and doers of ministry and missions, there are both those who

---

[1] Professor and Chairman, World Missions and Intercultural Studies, Dallas Theological Seminary. President, Evangelical Missiological Society.

[2] "Article II: Purpose." Constitution of the Evangelical Missiological Society.

practically discount the value of the sciences for missions and also those who make uncritical use of them.

Spiritual warfare advocates (a term I will use to include advocates of power encounter, territorial spirits, and spiritual mapping) believe they are rejecting what has become a predominantly scientific approach to missions in favor of supernatural dynamics. Concerned about the resistance that characterizes many of the last unreached peoples, they have concluded that demonic opposition has caused this phenomenon and that identification and binding of regional controlling spirits is the answer. This concept can be seen in the AD 2000 Prayer Track led by Peter and Doris Wagner and is fundamental to the "Light the Window" campaign in which one hundred "Gateway Cities" in the 10-40 window have been targeted for prayer visitation.[3]

Among missiologists inside and outside the EMS, the above mentioned developments find both enthusiastic support and emerging concern.[4] The EMS does not wish to polarize protagonists on either side, but calls all participants to constructive dialogue. As evangelicals, we share certain convictions. We all

- want to work for the completion of the Great Commission
- realize that unreached peoples generally constitute resistant groups
- believe Satan actively suppresses belief among non-Christians
- are eager for any breakthrough possible
- understand our real weapons are primarily spiritual
- believe the written Word of God should set the parameters for our belief and actions relative to the exercise of spiritual dynamics in ministry.

---

[3]Wagner, C. Peter, Stephen Peters, and Mark Wilson. *Praying Through the 100 Gateway Cities of the 10-40 Window*. Seattle, WA: YWAM Publications, 1995.

[4]*Evangelical Missions Quarterly* included two excellent articles that demonstrate the kind of help we can give each other through correction that comes from deeply committed, yet concerned, brethren. See Mike Wakely, "A Critical Look at a New 'Key' to Evangelization," and Tai M. Yip, "Spiritual Mapping: Another Approach," in *EMQ*, April 1995, pp. 152-170.

Nevertheless, there are differences. Most advocates of spiritual warfare believe all the above; but, in regard to the last, some emphasize the present reality of a spoken, non-normative revelation from God (a "word of wisdom"). This, they believe, is what enables them to understand issues about which there is a lack of written data in the Bible. They may also give considerable credence to data gained from dialogue with demonized people, believing that, through a command to tell the truth in Jesus' name, demons must divulge the truth.[5]

This epistemology tends to minimize the kind of systematic and rigorous observation of data that science normally implies. Some critics of the spiritual warfare approach have felt their concerns were trivialized by references to having been overwhelmed with Western rationalism.[6] On the other hand, the critics themselves have charged that a new animistic and syncretistic paradigm is emerging among spiritual warfare advocates.[7]

Debates like this need to find a safe haven free from animosity, offensiveness, and rancor. Hopefully, the EMS is such a place. To that end, we have encouraged and published a dialogue, *Spiritual Power and Missions: Raising the Issues,* and made it available to our membership at this conference.[8] This dialogue brings together the provocative paper by Robert J. Priest, Thomas Campbell, and Bradford A. Mullen, "Missiological Syncretism: The New Animistic Paradigm," presented at last year's EMS National Meeting. It includes responses by Charles Kraft and Patrick Johnstone and a summary by editor Ed Rommen.

---

[5]Wagner, C. Peter. "Territorial Spirits and World Missions." *EMQ,* July 1989, p. 284.

[6]Priest, Robert J., Thomas Campbell, and Bradford A. Mullen. "Missiological Syncretism: The New Animistic Paradigm." Paper presented to EMS National Meeting, November 1994, Chicago, IL. Now available in *Spiritual Power and Missions: Raising the Issues,* edited by Edward Rommen, Pasadena, CA: William Carey Library, 1995.

[7]Ibid.

[8]Rommen, Edward, ed. *Spiritual Power and Missions: Raising the Issues.* Pasadena, CA: William Carey Library, 1995.

Since all peoples and religions exhibit syncretism,[9] we should constantly be open to the possibility that we ourselves may be unduly, even unconsciously, influenced by non-Christian worldviews. As missiologists we will be open and non-defensive when held to account for the bases upon which we build or criticize mission strategy for the evangelical missions movement.

Returning to the more specific question of the relation of the social sciences to missiology, we should note James Scherer in his preface to the magnificent work by the late David Bosch, *Transforming Mission:*

> Missiologists know they need the other disciplines. And those in the other disciplines need missiology, perhaps more than they sometimes realize. Neither the insider's nor the outsider's view is complete in itself. . . . The complimentary relation between missiology and the other learned disciplines is a key of this series, and interaction will be its hallmark.[10]

Missiology is not simply *informed* by other scientific disciplines. It is by definition inclusive of the sciences. It is a discipline itself wherein theology; missionary experience; and the methods and insights of anthropology, sociology, psychology, communications, linguistics, demography, geography, and statistics are brought together for understanding and advancing the missionary enterprise.[11] Because of this, we are

---

[9]Van Rheenen, Gailyn. *Communicating Christ in Animistic Contexts.* Grand Rapids: Baker Book House, 1991, p. 96. Citing Timothy Warner, "Teaching Power Encounter," *Evangelical Missions Quarterly* 22 (January 1986): 66-71.

[10]Bosch, David. *Transforming Mission: Paradigm Shifts in Theology of Missions.* Maryknoll, NY: Orbis Books, 1993, p. xiv.

[11]Pentecost, Edward C. *Issues in Missiology: An Introduction.* Grand Rapids: Baker Book House, 1982, p. 10. I have added linguistics, demography, geography, and statistics to Pentecost's list, as it is clear to me these disciplines are also a part of missiology. See also James A. Scherer, "Missiology as a Discipline and What it Includes," *Missiology* 15:4 (October 1987): 507-22.

not debating *whether* the sciences relate, but *how* and *to what degree*.

Within the limits imposed by human nature, the sciences can illuminate missionary theology and practice and vice versa. Wycliffe Bible Translators is a good example of this symbiotic relationship. Their work has been greatly assisted by the sciences of cultural anthropology and linguistics. Having thus benefitted, Wycliffe (SIL) workers, after years of field experience and reflection, have become experts in both areas and have assumed professorships in those fields in several major universities.

The sciences, however, do not *make* things happen. They *describe* what happens, postulate and theorize on observed phenomena, and predict logical outcomes. Technology builds on science and obviously facilitates it, yet nothing save the Spirit of God can bring forth spiritual life where there has been none.

> The Spirit gives life; the flesh counts for nothing. The words I have spoken to you are spirit and they are life (Jn 6:33 NIV).

This fundamental truth of Scripture must surely keep us careful when applying insights from the sciences to the work of missions!

In spite of the fact that missiology presupposes the value of the sciences, there are many evangelicals who are wary of attempts to integrate the two. There are, of course, dangers. We tend to either reject the sciences or adopt and apply them with insufficient discrimination. Os Guiness notes:

> Since truth is truth, it would be odd for any Christian to deny the illuminating helpfulness of the social sciences. At the same time, however, it is amazing to witness the lemming-like rush of church leaders who forget theology in the charge after the latest insights of sociology— regardless of where the ideas come from or where they lead to. Carelessly handled,

innovation and adaptation become a form of corruption, capitulation, and idolatry.[12]

A kindred spirit, Mark Noll, in his lament on the disappearance of the American evangelical mind, complains that in the spiritual fervor (not necessarily because of it) of the late nineteenth century Holiness movement and the overlapping appearance of the Pentecostal, Fundamentalist, and Dispensational movements, an appreciation for nature and the value of science and the ability or willingness to take time to reflect deeply was lost.[13] Noll's criticism could be taken as supercilious and unwarranted. Indeed, Alister McGrath, in a dialogue between himself, Mark Noll, Richard Mouw, and Darrell Bock sponsored by *Christianity Today* in the summer of 1995, commented, "Mark does a good job of depicting how fundamentalists realized they had a problem on their hands and what they did in response, but, looking back, what else could they have done?"[14] Nevertheless, Noll's point of view needs careful consideration.

Noll's book *The Scandal of the Evangelical Mind* includes a chapter, "Thinking About Science," which is particularly apropos to our conference theme. There was a time, he maintains, when evangelicals valued the sciences and used them extensively to both understand Scripture better and appreciate the world around them. But as the nineteenth century drew to a close, a deep skepticism began to grow about the ability or interest of science to help the Christian cause. Evangelicals began to retreat from the universities or were marginalized by newly-monied titans of industry who wanted something else from the schools than the character formation the schools had hitherto held to be important.

---

[12]Guiness, Os and John Seel, eds. "Sounding Out the Idols of Church Growth," *No God But God: Breaking with the Idols of the Age.* Chicago: Moody Press, 1992, p. 157.

[13]Noll, Mark. *The Scandal of the Evangelical Mind.* Grand Rapids: Eerdmans, 1994.

[14]Noll, Mark, Alister McGrath, Richard Mouw, and Darrell Bock. "Scandal? A Forum on the Evangelical Mind." *Christianity Today,* August 14, 1995, p. 23. Noll reemphasizes his conviction that the world is a sacred object of study because God made it, entered it, and redeems it. Mouw says evangelicals are not against the mind, but the *mindset of the academy.*

For their part, evangelicals "dropped the Ninteenth Century conviction that the best theology should understand and incorporate the best science."[15] An antagonism to science began to flourish among evangelicals, and it was only insofar as science could be used to refute the opposition that evangelicals used it. What so deeply concerns Noll is that evangelical suspicion of the sciences led them to devalue even that which was the object of scientific study and its rigorous discipline of thought, namely, the world around them.

To Noll, both the world of nature and the human mind are supremely valuable. They are both creations of God. The former is worthy of study, and the latter is capable of that study. Worship of the Lord must include the sometimes forgotten element, the whole-hearted use of the mind (Mt 22:37).[16]

Distrust of intellectual exercises and the sciences led evangelicals in two directions. On the one hand they moved to an intuitive way of knowing rather than a way of careful deduction. Their convictions either came directly from Scripture or from the Holy Spirit or an intuitive sense of what they should believe or do. Later, when they felt more comfortable with the sciences, having reaped many happy benefits from its application in daily life, they began to use science, but in an unreflective, selective, and hurried way. As Noll says, ". . . if evangelicals are ever to cultivate the mind, habits of intuitionism—or the rapid movement from first impressions to final conclusions—must be changed."[17]

Noll's chapter "Thinking About the Sciences" is really a call to scrutinize the "two books" of God's revelation: The written Scriptures and the book of Nature. Charles Hodge makes Noll's point for him when he says, "Nature is as truly a revelation of God as the Bible; and we only interpret the Word of God by the Word of God when we interpret the Bible by science."[18]

---

[15]Noll, *The Scandal of the Evangelical Mind*, p. 185.

[16]Ibid, p. 7 and p. 23, citing Os Guiness, "Persuasion for the New World: An Interview with Os Guiness," in *Crucible* 4:2 (Summer 1992): 15.

[17]Ibid, p. 245.

[18]Ibid, p. 183, citing Charles Hodge, "The Bible in Science," *New York Observer*, March 26, 1863, pp. 98-99.

Hodge goes on to argue that, since all of nature is of God, the observation of it will lead to understandings applicable to Scripture, and Scripture will lead to understanding nature better. This is probably an overly-sanguine hope, given the impaired capabilities of unregenerate men. But perhaps both Noll and Hodge before him were thinking mainly of Christian scientists.

None of us doubt the reality that nature constitutes a testament to the glorious existence and reality of God. The Bible directly says that "the heavens declare the glory of God" (Ps 19), but science is not a purely objective observation of nature. Scientists have their presuppositions, as objective as they may try to make them.

All this brings to mind the issue of natural, or general, revelation and the possibility of deriving a "natural theology" from it. This question was debated earlier this century by Karl Barth and Emil Brunner and has implications for missiology. Barth concluded in the strongest possible terms, "Nien!" ("No!") to the possibility of a natural theology.[19] This conclusion would apply both to attempts to draw the knowledge of God from scientific observation of the world, unaided by Scripture, and in our day to attempts by regional theologians to construct African, Latin American, or Asian theologies strictly from observations of their cultures and histories. It naturally has a bearing on the question of whether we can construct theologies or mission strategy from observing and listening to demons as well.

The Apostle Paul makes it clear in Romans 1:18-32 that, while God revealed himself in creation, no one draws correct conclusions from it. He further says in 1 Corinthians 2:6-16 that, insofar as the knowledge of *God* is concerned, natural, or unregenerate, people can never independently perceive the truth. However, Paul distinguishes between knowledge about God and knowledge about humanity and concludes that humans can attain true insights about humanity apparently unaided by the Spirit of God (1Co 2:11). This gives at least a window of opportunity for the sciences!

It is the understanding of the limitations of humanity the observer that makes evangelicals wary of the scientists'

---

[19]Brunner, Emil and Karl Barth. "No! Answer to Emil Brunner." In *Natural Theology*. London: Centenary, 1946. Reprinted by University Microfilms International, Ann Arbor, Michigan and London, 1979.

ability to deliver insights about God's world or work. And, if we are more activist than reflective, should we beat our breasts about it?

I believe that Noll fails to fully appreciate the legitimate urgency that significant Bible doctrines, not proof texts, give to the work of God. Why does he assail Dispensationalism alone for producing the apocalyptic sense that Christ could come at any moment and that, therefore, lengthy intellectual reflection may be a luxury we cannot afford? Christ himself makes clear and the apostles teach that he may return at any moment and bring to a close the present age (Mt 24-25; 1Th 5:1-3). While Peter agrees with Jesus that time for God is a relative matter and we should avoid the setting of dates, he tells us in 2 Peter 3:3-15 that a normal response to the approach of the Lord's coming is to concern oneself with personal holiness and expectancy, considering that time itself goes on for salvation purposes.

Why does it seem strange or lamentable that so many evangelicals are impatient with contemplation and intellectualizing? Have they not been taught by Scriptures to be wary? Ah well . . . there are other threads of God's wisdom to be woven into this tapestry. "Be still and know that I am God. I will be exalted among the nations, I will be exalted in the earth" (Ps 46:10 NIV). "Be still before the Lord and wait patiently for him, do not fret" (Ps 37:7 NIV).

Is there any way to synthesize the urgency of our task with patient trust in a seemingly unhurried God? Perhaps like Henri Nouwen we should head for Daybreak via Trosly, France. Maybe there is yet hope that we can combine dynamic service with inner stillness, as he has apparently done. It's probably worth it—both for the cause of Christ and our palpitating hearts!

Along the way, let's pause, and think, and read from the two books about which Mark Noll so eloquently writes: the world of God's creation (Ps 19) and the Word of God's writing (2Ti 3:16-17). The Spirit and the gifts are ours, as Luther put it. As long as we don't try to construct missiology like a natural theology derived from general revelation alone, we should be safe![20] So, onward to the further contemplation of the relation between missiology and the social sciences!

---

[20]Ibid.

One final word of encouragement. If you find yourself among the groups criticized by Mark Noll for contributing to the decline of evangelical intellectual life, take heart from this: As missiologists we stand among those approved by our brother. As Noll looks for signs of hope, it is you that he sees. Listen to this as you ponder the question of missiology and the social sciences:

> Evangelical activism also has a fuller potential for sustaining the life of the mind than the evangelical history of North America might at first suggest. . . . When missiologists—often trained by evangelicals and sponsored by evangelicals—study what happens when evangelicals communicate the gospel cross-culturally, the result is a stunning series of theologically grounded insights. . . . Their work, in short, produces exactly the vantage point for differentiating between distinctive cultural expressions of Christianity and essential Christian expressions in a given culture that evangelicalism has long required. It is more fitting than ironic that one of the most important products of evangelical missionary efforts may be to teach missionary-sending evangelicals how to use the gospel they proclaim as a means of thought.[21]

---

[21]Noll, *The Scandal of the Evangelical Mind*, pp.251-252.

## REFERENCE LIST

Constitution of the Evangelical Missiological Society

Bosch, David

    1993    *Transforming Mission: Paradigm Shifts in Theology of Missions.* Maryknoll, NY: Orbis Books.

Brunner, Emil and Karl Barth

    1979    "No! Answer to Emil Brunner." *Natural Theology.* London: Centenary, 1946. Reprinted by University Microfilms International, Ann Arbor, Michigan and London.

Guiness, Os and John Seel, eds.

    1992    "Sounding Out the Idols of Church Growth." *No God But God: Breaking with the Idols of the Age.* Chicago: Moody Press.

Noll, Mark

    1994    *The Scandal of the Evangelical Mind.* Grand Rapids: Eerdmans.

Noll, Mark, Alister McGrath, Richard Mouw, and Darrell Bock

    1995    "Scandal? A Forum on the Evangelical Mind." *Christianity Today,* August 14.

Pentecost, Edward C.

    1982    *Issues in Missiology: An Introduction.* Grand Rapids: Baker Book House.

Priest, Robert J., Thomas Campbell, and Bradford A. Mullen

    1995    "Missiological Syncretism: The New Animistic Paradigm." Paper presented to EMS National Meeting, November 1994, Chicago, IL. Now available in *Spiritual Power and Missions: Raising the Issues,* edited by Edward Rommen, Pasadena, CA: William Carey Library.

Rommen, Edward, ed.

    1995    *Spiritual Power and Missions: Raising the Issues.* Pasadena, CA: William Carey Library.

Scherer, James A.

    1987    "Missiology as a Discipline and What it Includes." *Missiology* 15:4 (October).

\_\_\_\_\_ and Stephen B. Bevans, eds.

    1994    *New Directions in Mission and Evangelization 2: Theological Foundations.* Maryknoll, NY: Orbis Books.

Van Rheenen, Gailyn

    1991    *Communicating Christ in Animistic Contexts.* Grand Rapids: Baker Book House.

Wagner, C. Peter

    1989    "Territorial Spirits and World Missions." *EMQ,* July.

Wagner, C, Peter, Stephen Peters, and Mark Wilson

    1995    *Praying Through the 100 Gateway Cities of the 10-40 Window.* Seattle, WA: YWAM Publications.

Wakely, Mike

    1995    "A Critical Look at a New 'Key' to Evan-gelization." *EMQ,* April.

Yip, Tai M.

    1995    "Spiritual Mapping: Another Approach." *EMQ,* April.

# 2

# SOCIOLOGY AND MISSIOLOGY: REFLECTIONS ON MISSION RESEARCH

## Gary R. Corwin[1]

### INTRODUCTION

Two decades of mission research for mobilization and strategy have revealed that it has many faces. It can be good. It can be bad. And it can be, well, aesthetically challenging, to coin a politically correct euphemism. What is the measure of each description? The point of view of this paper is that it is good when it is well-grounded theologically, its methodology is appropriate, it reflects God's passion for taking the gospel to the lost, and it actually furthers the cause of world evangelization, particularly to the least reached.

It is bad when it is based on assumptions that are weak theologically and/or logically, when it projects wrong motives on others without first walking in their shoes, or when it actually discourages the pursuit of biblical mandates because they are not one's own particular priorities.

It is aesthetically challenging when its goals and assumptions are good but its methodology is flawed to the point that the message conveyed actually leads to less accuracy and clarity, greater confusion, and produces mixed results in terms of its impact in world evangelization.

The great divide in assessment, to put things another way, is over the faithfulness of research and its assumptions to the foundations laid for it in Scripture, and over the validity of

---

[1] Gary Corwin works for the Society for International Ministries (SIM) and is an associate editor of the *Evangelical Missions Quarterly*.

its methodology both technically and in light of the mandates of Scripture.

So what really is research in a biblical and mission context? It is interesting to note that research in the Scriptures was seldom if ever undertaken for the purpose of showing how doable a task was. Rather it was usually an activity commanded by the Lord to make clear the magnitude of that which God was about to accomplish for his people, thus maximizing his glory in the doing of it.

If one looks carefully at the spying out of the land of Canaan as recorded in Numbers 13 (the archetypal model for mission research), one quickly sees that the debate was not between those who said that the task was of a manageable size and was therefore doable, and those who said that it was not. Rather the debate was between those who agreed that the challenge was enormous and beyond them (v.v. 32-33, "The land we explored devours those living in it . . . We seemed like grasshoppers").

Note that Joshua and Caleb never questioned their colleagues' descriptions of their very formidable Canaanite enemies, but rather pointed at the same time to the all-sufficient strength and mercy of God on their behalf (Nu 14:8-9, "If the Lord is pleased with us, he will lead us into the land . . . . Their protection is gone, but the Lord is with us. Do not be afraid of them"). Yes, the battle is winnable, but only because God is doing it. Still today God's people must beware of being drawn in by either of two dangerous opinions regarding the value of research. One is based in excessive optimism ("We can do it!"), while the other is based in excessive negativism ("It can't be done!"). The correct view, of course, is more doxological ("God can do it!").

The problems with our research are not just theological, however. They are also methodological. "A generation after Marshall McLuhan, the Church still behaves as if the forms of culture, especially the forms of mass media and the role they play in our lives, are value-neutral." So says Kenneth A. Myers in his excellent book *All God's Children and Blue Suede Shoes: Christians and Popular Culture* (Crossway, 1989). This statement applies no less tellingly to the church's (and particularly the mission community's) love affair with research and analysis based upon the tools and techniques of information science, quantitative analysis, and marketing, than it does the stalwarts of popular culture, television and music.

Fortunately, the impact of such research and analysis is at its worse more benign than either television or music is today, and at its best a real boon to the missionary enterprise. There are enough pluses, minuses, and challenges in this cutting-edge endeavor, however, to warrant a careful assessment. It is the only way really to maximize the benefits, minimize the negatives, and to respond to the challenges in a successful fashion.

The problems that do exist, of course, do not stem from change and innovation in themselves. The missions community has always been at the forefront of technological and methodological innovation. Many new approaches in areas like medicine, education, media, and even transportation can be traced directly to the creative genius of missionaries seeking to harness or customize the best tools available for the sake of fulfilling the Great Commission. Rather, they stem from embracing the forms and technologies of modern culture without reflecting carefully on the dangers, as well as the benefits, inherent in them. Such reflection is a significant purpose of this paper.

## THE GOOD

When in 1974 Dr. Ralph Winter gave his famous speech, "The Highest Priority: Cross-Cultural Evangelism," at the first Lausanne Congress on World Evangelization, a new era in mission history was begun. It was not really so much that a new vision was born, but that a new way of looking at an old vision was provided. This focus breathed new life and a new sense of imperative into the very old biblical task of taking the gospel to the unreached where they are least reached. This had been the watchword of the faith missions movement which pioneered the taking of the gospel to the inland areas, but it can be traced throughout the church's history wherever it was actively engaged in pursuing the Father's will to spread his kingdom "to the uttermost parts of the earth." What was new at Lausanne was that for the first time in the modern period the task was now couched primarily in terms of *ethne* or peoples, and religious blocks, rather than in geographic or geo-political terms.

Over the last two decades since that speech an astounding shift has taken place. The concept of unreached peoples (in contrast to unreached people) is on the lips of virtually everyone concerned with the mission of Christ's church. The 1991 encyclical *Redemptoris Missio*, issued by John Paul II, is elegant testimony to just how far the concept has come. This has been a remarkable boon to world evangelization, reflected in the strategic outreach planning of agencies and churches, and in the mobilization of new resources to see the task completed.

A review of the positive developments over this period is an exhilarating experience. For example, who can assess the true impact of focused prayer for the least reached that has been stimulated by Patrick Johnstone's *Operation World* through its several editions since 1978. Or who can know how many church bodies around the globe have been jump-started to new outreach among the least reached through the seminars and workshops of John Robb of MARC, or John's book *The Power of People Group Thinking*. And on the list could go, of vision-expanding contributions through the prolific writings of people like David Barrett, through the unparalleled historical research of the *International Bulletin of Missionary Research*, or the research/mobilization work of ministries at the USCWM, or of the Adopt-A-People Clearinghouse. And all of that is not to mention the scores of grassroots research projects undertaken by mission agencies and church bodies to identify the least reached, to document the resources available to meet them, and to determine the best strategies to reach them.

This list could go on and on, and the hearts of God's people should be thrilled with all that has been accomplished. Peoples, priorities, and prayer have taken their rightful place at the forefront of focus, the direct result of the enormous effort that has been expended over this period to use research and analysis in the cause of world evangelization.

## THE BAD

In addition to all that has been so positive in the new emphasis on research and analysis in mission, it must be admitted that there has also been a downside. At the top of the list in importance has been a de-emphasis and a diminution of theology in some quarters, as something unessential at best, or counterproductive at worse. The end goals of evangelization and mobilization have at times become the measure of all things, it would seem.

Not altogether unexpectedly, logic has also suffered, and with it a generosity of spirit with regard to the motives of others and the mandates of God. Singleness of purpose has at times degenerated into tunnel vision.

Without doubt the most serious affront has been in sloughing off as unimportant that most basic of questions, "What does it mean to be a Christian?" Is calling oneself a Christian all that is necessary? This was the fatal flaw in the work of Edinburgh 1910 and it is a mistake being made in the thinking of many today. The furor caused in the last two years by the document *Evangelicals and Catholics Together: The Christian Mission in the Third Millennium* is testimony to that fact. Missiologically the question really boils down to whether countries like France, Greece, or Argentina are legitimate foci for evangelical missions or not. How one answers this question, of course, makes a vast difference in how one assesses the quality of our mission deployments today.

To put the theological point even more directly, "Just how important is justification by faith *alone*?" One of the great benefits of the recent furor has been the able articulation of all that is embodied in scriptural teaching on this most essential Reformation principle of saving faith, too long taken for granted by too many. Where we have been weak on this central point of Christian theology, our mission strategies and the research assumptions that undergird them have been seriously flawed. While there is some value in pointing out the distinction between those geographic areas where people at least name the name of Christ in some fashion, and those places where they do not, this is neither an adequate criterion for measuring the completion of the task, nor the scope of our responsibility. The idea that one should disparage part of God's mandate in order to highlight another area which has been too long neglected is neither good analysis nor good Christianity.

Another theological foundation which has suffered in recent research paradigms has to do with the nature of the missionary task. The essence of the problem is that the task of missions is seen only in terms of evangelism or church planting, rather than the biblical standard of disciple-making. This too has great bearing on how one views current missionary activity and deployment. Much of the current research and analysis consistently understates the disciple-making task of the church ("baptize . . . teaching them to obey everything I have commanded you") as outlined in the Great Commission. Data then gathered or explained on the premise that another activity is the focus of the task (even when that other activity is something exceptionally good which does constitute part of the task, like evangelism or church planting) leads to wrong conclusions and confusion.

Flowing then from wrong assumptions about who is a Christian, and what constitutes the missionary task, come conclusions that project wrong motives on others (without first walking in their shoes), or which discourage the pursuit of biblical mandates that do not match up to one's own particular priorities. It has been argued, for example, that agencies have been untrue to their original charters as pioneer missions, and that the least reached peoples of the earth remain that way because of the indifference or misguided priorities of mission agencies.

Although genuine loss of outreach vision does sometimes occur, even among mission agencies, the generalized concerns expressed on this point overstate the case. For the majority of mission agencies trying to do their job well, taking the accusation seriously and to its logical conclusion would present something of a Catch-22 situation. The moment an agency engages in a ministry to one of the least reached peoples of the earth, that people group immediately becomes less needy than other groups; and that agency, in the convoluted logic of the argument, becomes something less than truly "pioneer."

For some of the agencies the accusation leveled is really based on disagreement concerning the worthiness of their ministry target. Missions established over the last century and more with the express purpose of outreach to the christo-pagan millions of South America, for example, have certainly been true to their charters, even if some choose to view those charters as mistaken.

The bottom line in much research has too often revealed the unfortunate tendency to draw the boundaries of the global missionary task around what has been done among a people, rather than on what remains to be done. Thus a checklist mentality often dominates which has an overwhelming bias toward being able to describe certain tasks as completed and certain people groups as reached, whether or not they really are.

The result is that rather than focusing on the spectrum of tasks which making disciples entails, and rejoicing in the deployment of God's servants in performing those tasks, the constant rejoinder is an accusation of improper deployment. The fact is that with rare exceptions we do not need less missionaries where they are. We simply need more where they are not.

## THE AESTHETICALLY CHALLENGING

Research becomes aesthetically challenging when, though goals and assumptions may be good, its methodology is flawed to the point that the message conveyed actually leads to less accuracy and clarity, greater confusion, and produces mixed results in terms of its impact in world evangelization. The issue really boils down to what users and sub-users think is true after they have interacted with a presentation of data. Is their understanding likely to be a true and accurate reflection of reality, or will it be skewed because of weakness in the underlying terminology and assumptions?

Definitions have been particularly troublesome and untidy in the mission arena over the last two decades. Each researcher (and mobilizer), it seems has, had his or her own nuance for key words, which is often at variance with the way they are used by other researchers, and rarely the same way that they are understood by most Christians. A prime example is the word "evangelized."

What happens when words like this one, which we all know and understand in a general way, are redefined for a technical usage which few of us understand, but many of us hear about? The short answer is confusion. Most of you would be surprised, I suspect, to read as I did in a prayer league's annual report that Bangladesh is 46% evangelized, India is 72% evangelized, and Pakistan is 48% evangelized. Full stop. The figures, of course, came from a widely known researcher who uses the term "evangelized" in a very specific way.

What may be fine for the internally consistent use of the data based on the researcher's assumptions, ends up playing havoc in the broader Christian community when used without detailed explanation. While there is nothing inherently wrong in the process, one has to wonder about the wisdom of co-opting benchmark Christian terms for such purposes. Why not forget the shorthand terms altogether and simply describe precisely what our numbers mean in such instances? The seeming answer to that is that we are so enamored with precision, or at least the appearance of precision, that we force soft data into frameworks that make us look good ("Only a researcher can understand this"). Unfortunately, it also leaves the serious reader scratching his or her head about our meaning, and the casual reader or hearer with a wrong impression.

Another prime example is the use of the term "unreached peoples." This all-important term implies a division of the world into two parts —reached peoples and unreached peoples. This is fair enough, as far as it goes. What occurs, however, is a loss of theological and missiological clarity in the use of this term, as well as other key terms dependent on it. And because "unreached" is used in so many contexts, confusion often reigns. Add to that the fact that such basic terms as "mission" and "missions" are built upon a definition of the unreached, and the problem is compounded further.

Yet another example is the contrast between "frontier" and "regular" missions. Is this kind of contrast a fair one, or does it convey a high octane / low octane scenario before the first word of definition is even spoken? Who gets excited about regular anything? Parallelism and fairness might argue instead for contrasting "frontier" and "discipling" missionary efforts, pointing out that both are part of the overall missionary task to "make disciples of all nations."

## CONCLUSION: SIGNS OF HOPE, AND HAZARDS AHEAD

Mission research and analysis for mobilization and global strategy has made a difference over the last two decades, most of it for good and for clarity, but some of it not so good and not so clear. Where it has not been scrupulous about theological or methodological integrity it has not been particularly helpful. Where it has, the dividends have been significant. As we look toward the future from our current vantage point we can see both signs of hope, and hazards that remain. Interestingly, the greatest hazards are usually the flip side of the greatest signs of hope. We will conclude by detailing several of these:

> 1. *There is hope in the heightened cooperation exhibited by researchers, exemplified perhaps best by the joint efforts of the Peoples Information Network or PIN Group.* \* *There is hazard in the continuing tendency to provide precise-sounding answers based on unsubstantiated, insufficient, or soft data.*

Perhaps the greatest guarantor of methodological reliability is that the thesis is testable, or minimally, that at least the thought processes of the researcher are both revealed and reproducible by others. If the users are expected to simply accept the end product by faith, there is something terribly wrong. A community of peers who work out of the same data pool, and wrestle together with the all-important definitional and assumption issues, is essential to the end products being credible and on target.

The danger in this new age of the "infomercial" is that the lines between reliable research and mobilization rhetoric are sometimes blurred. Truth issues are replaced by perception ones. Those who have the numbers and the media to present them often win the battle of persuasion, whether the numbers are reliable or not.

> 2. *There is hope in the growing recognition that theology and how we use words matters, even in our assumptions for research. There is hazard in the number who still do not think so, or who at least function in such a way as to lead one to that conclusion.*

As has been emphasized above, our research must be the servant of our theology, not the reverse. Many seem to be reaffirming this in many different contexts, and this is as it should be. We must beware, however, lest our theological commitments cease to inform our research praxis. I have a friend who is a good scholar and fine missiologist, but exhibits this

---

\*The body includes groups like the Adopt-A-People Clearinghouse, Wycliff Bible Translators, the AD 2000 Movement, the Foreign Mission Board of the Southern Baptist Convention, Global Mapping International, and others.

tendency. In a response to an inquiry from me he wrote as follows, "Yes, we should have a strong statement of faith. It should be biblical, evangelical, and Reformation-based, but, to repeat, I do not believe that our doctrinal statement should be used as a benchmark to measure whether a given group is reached or unreached. That has been clearly defined in our frontier missiology." While I can understand his passion as a researcher to stick with those things which are clearer and more easily measurable, I simply do not believe that the goal of having clean numbers justifies ignoring that which is central to the Scripture, nor is it worth the confusion, disincentive, and division it creates among God's people.

> 3. *There is hope in a maturing concept of mission research as a servant of ministry rather than a surrogate profession. There is hazard in the tendency to use it as a substitute for dependency on God or for doing our part.*

Research makes a valuable contribution to defining the scope of any task. It makes it possible to avoid a lot of wasted effort. But, having said that, in God's economy it does not rank as high as at least two other things. The first of these is the preparation of the doers.

It might be helpful to imagine research and analysis as matching the role played by military intelligence in a war, i.e. determining the scope of the task and the strength of the enemy. The preparation of the doers on this analogy would be comparable to the physical, mental and psychological preparation that soldiers go through. It is possible to know all about your enemy, but not have prepared resources to do anything about it. With regard to the war for world evangelization, E. M Bounds' classic statement perhaps says it best, "The Church is looking for better methods. God is looking for better men."

The second of the things more important than research and analysis is the actual fighting of the war. It is possible to fight and even win a war with a very inadequate definition of what will be required, but no war has ever been won by research, analysis, and planning alone. There must be an engaging in the battle.

A friend told me once about a course he took on ornithology, or the study of birds. He shared how the class had visited a nature reserve in Michigan in order to see the endangered Kirtland Warbler. On arrival they had been linked up in a guided group with other bird watchers from another place. The purpose of the visit was to not only see this species of bird, but to learn all they could about it and to become trained in the methods of assisting such endangered species. It came as quite a surprise to them, therefore, when having finally spotted a Kirtland Warbler, their new-found associates in the group were eager to move on in search of the Canadian Warbler. The difference is that these others were "listers," as they are called in bird-watching circles, and not "doers." Eager to identify and classify, but slow to do the thing most needed. Which are we, and which will characterize mission research in the next two decades?

# 3

# THE CONTRIBUTION OF CULTURAL ANTHROPOLOGY TO MISSIOLOGY

## Norman E. Allison[1]

Alan R. Tippet defines *missiology* as

> The academic discipline or science which researches, records, and applies data relating to the biblical origin, the history . . . , the anthropological principles and techniques, and the theological base of the Christian mission (1987:xiii).

Other writers add or subtract from this list of disciplines involved in missiology, but cultural anthropology has always been recognized as a vital component. It is these cultural "anthropological principles and techniques" which this study will attempt to broadly delineate as they have impacted the discipline of missiology.[2] In this study, theology, anthropology, and missions will be seen as interrelated closely in the development of missiology.

It should be noted that *anthropology* is usually divided into four sub-fields: archaeology, linguistics, physical and

---

[1] Professor of Cultural Anthropology at Taccoa Falls College.

[2] The nature of this study precludes developing the contributions of cultural anthropology to missiology at much more than a cursory level; however, the attached bibliography will serve the reader who wishes to have a deeper understanding of the issues. There is a sense in which the other behavioral sciences are to be included within the category of "anthropology," since by definition anthropology is holistic in drawing upon psychology, sociology, etc.

cultural anthropology. The unifying concern of these four very different specializations is the human being and his culture. From this point on, the subfield *cultural anthropology* will most often be referred to generically as *anthropology*.

At present, *anthropology*-related courses are a significant part of majors offered at a number of Bible colleges and seminaries for people preparing for missionary service, but this has not always been the case. In speaking of the contribution of cultural anthropology to missiology, it must be recognized that the relationship between theologians and anthropologists has been, and continues to be, though to a lesser degree than in the past, a "love/hate relationship" (Hiebert 1978). Perhaps in large part due to an ongoing mistrust of the potential secularizing influence of anthropology, a true partnership between these fields which are foundational to the discipline of missiology has been much later in coming than might have been. Nevertheless, especially in the last thirty years, the contribution of anthropology to the developing discipline of missiology has been significant. A major reason this has been true is a tribute to *Christian* anthropologists and missionaries[3] who applied cross-cultural methodology from a Christian worldview to the communication of the gospel in our diverse world.

The first connection between anthropology and missions seems to have come through descriptive linguistics, which found a vital role in Bible translation (Hiebert 1994:9). Some of the same men, E. A. Nida, W. A. Smalley, J. A. Loewen, W. D. Reyburn, and others, also promoted an understanding of anthropology and its value to the broader missionary task, in large part, through the stimulus and insights of their writings in the journal *Practical Anthropology*. For nineteen years (1953-1972) this bimonthly journal provided a forum for the widespread communication of research in anthropology and its practical application in Christian missions. Many of its readers were

---

[3]In dealing with the contributions of anthropologists to missiology, it should also be emphasized that missionaries have made tremendous contributions to anthropology. The most obvious area is in the area of linguistics (Summer Institute of Linguistics and Wycliffe Bible Translators), but missionary scholarship in the areas of ethnography, in particular, has impacted anthropology since its development as a behavioral science. Anthropologist Roger M. Keesing traces this indebtedness to "an old and enduring tradition of missionary scholarship" (1976:459).

field missionaries, and direct practical applications were obvious to those "in the trenches," putting theory into practice.

Alan Tippett was another noteworthy anthropologist who, through his writing (see bibliography) and his teaching at Fuller School of World Mission, did much to reinforce this same openness toward cultures, and toward cultural anthropology in particular.

Cultural anthropology, as a *behavioral science*, deals not only with what people *say* they do and believe, but with what they *actually* do and think. It is concerned with the description and analysis of people's lives and traditions. The applied scientific analysis of human behavior and beliefs has given to those who would communicate Christ in different cultures a tool of incalculable value.[4]

The best vantage point from which to view the contribution of cultural anthropology to missiology is through an understanding of the concept of *culture*. According to Louis Luzbetak, the "understanding of culture is . . . anthropology's most significant contribution to missiology" (1993:133).

The influential American anthropologist Franz Boas championed the concept of culture for understanding human diversity. He argued that culture was distinct from biological "race" or language. Culture has been broadly defined as the "pattern of life within a community—the regularly recurring activities and material and social arrangements" characteristic of a particular human group (Goodenough 1961:521). Culture is seen as an all-pervasive thing by which all of human behavior is systematized and through which it is structured and learned. But in another, deeper sense, we have come to know that culture is also to be understood as "an organized system of knowledge and belief" (Keesing 1976:138) and in this sense *culture* refers to the realm of ideas, beliefs and values.

My own introduction to the concept of culture came from an initial exposure to anthropology through the book *Customs and Cultures* (1954) by Eugene Nida.[5] I have no doubt that I was

---

[4]In a brief survey of Christian anthropologists, there was a general consensus regarding the importance of the contributions which are highlighted in this study.

[5]In 1957 when I entered Toccoa Falls College to prepare for missionary service, I had never so much as thought of culture or anthropology as a part of that process. There was no major in missiology then, but I did

not the only one in late 1950s and early 1960s who was influenced by this highly readable introductory volume. We, in those years of missionary preparation, were exposed for the first time to the exciting mysteries of cultures around the world. Anthropology, at the same time, came a step closer to missiology as a developing science.[6]

In addition, as cultural awareness continued to develop among missionaries, we became more sensitive to *the cross-cultural perspective*. Anthropology tends to generalize about human behavior on the basis of data from many cultures. Moreover, anthropology stipulates that any generalization about human nature has to be shown to be true in a wide variety of different cultures if it is to be accepted. The paradox of culture, however, is that, as we humans learn to accept our own cultural beliefs and values, we unconsciously learn to reject those of other peoples. At birth, we are predisposed to learning culture and language (Chomsky 1957, 1968). This predisposition is reinforced as we grow and are taught by our parents, our schools, and our society what is proper and improper, good and evil, acceptable and unacceptable behavior. At the subconscious level, we learn the symbolic meanings of behavior and through them interpret the meaning of actions. We are thus enculturated into a monocultural view of reality, and our vision is limited to this narrow perspective.

Anthropology has understood this phenomenon and has countered its ethnocentric bias with a different view of other cultures. This has occured through the development of a research methodology, fundamental to the anthropologist's approach to any new culture, known as *participant-observation*. This method involves learning a people's culture through direct participation in their everyday life over an extended period of

---

take the few "missions" courses offered to those who would be missionaries. One of these required courses was Cultural Anthropology, and our textbook was *Customs and Cultures* by Eugene Nida. Through this new understanding in the minds of missionary candidates like myself, later to be a field missionary, and then a professional anthropologist, cultural anthropology was evolving as a significant segment of the science of missiology.

[6]Further development of the concept of culture, with its many implications for missiology, is summarized well in the writings of Luzbetak (1993) and Hiebert (1985).

time (Haviland 1993:13). Many field missionaries, with their goal of reaching people for Christ in a second culture, have found this tool of research a primary means for understanding those whom God has called them to serve. The resulting ethnographic studies of specific cultures by anthropologists, and missionaries with anthropological training, have given us a broad range of cultural information which today forms a significant data base for the analysis of specific societies.

In addition, this type of first-hand involvement in a second culture is directly related to the incarnational role modeled by the apostle Paul in "... becoming all things to all men so that by all possible means I might save some" (1 Co 9:22 NIV).

> Incarnational witness goes where people are, speaks their language and becomes one with them as far as we are psychologically able and our consciences allow. People need to hear the gospel in their heart language and see it lived out by us (Hiebert 1994:66).

Anthropology has, in addition, enabled missiologists to know that each culture has its own *worldview*. We know that in every culture there are assumptions made about the nature of reality and about the nature of a person, his relations with other people, and his place in what he defines as *his world*. Paul Bohannan writes:

> A worldview provides a people with a structure of reality; defines, classifies, and orders the *"really real"* in the universe, in their world, and in their society.... Religion provides a people with their fundamental orientation toward that reality... (1992:234 quoting Oritz).

Studies of worldview have taken us even deeper in our awareness that beliefs, values, and symbols must be understood within the context of a particular culture. This research methodology has focused attention on the implicit and explicit assumptions that underlie specific beliefs and norms of a people group. Such investigation has probed even into a society's conception of reality and its view of the end and purpose of human life.

Anthropologist George Foster, for example, found a distinctive cognitive orientation and ideology (*worldview*) which characterized certain peasant econmies (1965, 1969). From several ethnographic cases, he illustrated a concept he identified as the *image of limited good*, referring to the assumption that "all desired things in life . . . exist in finite and unexpandable quantities" (1969:83). This meant that a wealthy peasant, for example, was gaining his wealth at the expense of his less fortunate neighbors. For this reason, if one were to have more wealth, it should be hidden from others. The concept of worldview focuses attention on these types of human beliefs and values at the deepest levels, the very areas of life to which Christianity is directed (Kraft 1995).

Another of the important areas of contribution from anthropology, developing particularly from communication theory, is that of *cross-cultural communication*. Mayers writes that

> Anthropologists have contributed significantly to the sub-discipline Cross-cultural Communication and these foundational studies have benefited numerous missiologists who got into the field at a later date. Most of the training of missiologists and missionaries rests strongly, in the 80's and 90's, on foundations . . . laid in the 50's . . . 60's . . . and 70's (1995).

The expanding bibliography of books on cross-cultural (*intercultural*) communication reveals that literature on the subject is rather extensive. Among the most noteworthy have been the works of Eugene Nida, Marvin Mayers, Charles Kraft, and David Hesselgrave.

The development of comparative cultural analysis in cross-cultural methodology has also benefited greatly from a model given originally by Kenneth Pike (1954),[7] contrasting the *etic and emic perspectives*. The *emic* perspective is understood as the insider's viewpoint, the participant in a given culture. The *etic* view is that of the outside analyst, developing categories and distinctions based on his view of culture. As anthropolo-

---

[7] This model is still explained in contemporary secular anthropology texts (Bodley 1994) and has been used in missiological literature by Kraft (1979), Hiebert (1983) and others.

gists work to discover, and then to predict patterns of human behavior, this model has helped greatly in differentiating the way people see themselves from the way they are seen by outsiders. For example, the etic view of a particular illness may be explained by the outsider according to germ theories. The insider's explanation (emic) may understand the same illness in terms of activity in the spiritual realms of witchcraft, sorcery, ghosts, spirits, and sin (Hess 1983:253-4). Knowing that cultures differ, not only in the ideas that people have, but in the conceptual categories they use, has led missiology into a much deeper understanding of important cultural variations.

Jacob Loewen writes of a situation in which very different worldviews actually cause different groups of people to hear a different content from the same message. He says that in order to prove this point to a group of doubtful, seminary-trained missionaries working in Africa, he asked both missionaries and nationals to write down what they thought was the central message of certain [Bible] stories.

> The first example was the story of Joseph. The missionaries wrote that here was a man who was loyal to God even to the point of resisting the most fierce of sexual temptations. The Africans wrote that here was a man who was totally loyal to his family. In spite of the fact that his brothers had mistreated him, he remained loyal to them even when he occupied the royal throne in Egypt (1979:160-61).

Anthropologists believe that other societies deserve to be studied and understood without being prejudged through one's own beliefs and values. This perspective, known as *cultural relativism*, proposes that as people in another society are studied "[their] moral and aesthetic ideas must not be evaluated by the norms of the observer's own culture, but must instead be understood and appreciated in their cultural context" (Hunter and Whitten 1976:102). This concept (judging from missiological literature) is often understood differently by nonanthropologists.[8] Christian anthropologists recognize that, pursued to its logical end, ethical relativism would be the final outcome of cultural relativism. They have, for this reason, sought to use the valuable aspects of this perspective while being careful to recognize the dangers.

Help has come to many from a text widely used in seminaries and Bible colleges, Marvin Mayers' *Christianity Confronts Culture* (1974). Here he develops the concept of *biculturalism*. Seeing the value of cultural relativism for viewing cultures more objectively, and at the same time being aware of the inherent dangers of ethical relativism, Mayers explains:

> The monocultural approach to the behavior of others is to see in what ways that behavior . . . can be changed to conform to the expectations of the one viewing it. The crosscultural or bicultural approach lets man be man and God be God in evaluating behavior. Thus, biblical absolutism is teamed with cultural relativism. . . . A truly bicultural individual can introduce the Gospel in any culture or subculture without the accompanying 'cultural baggage' that is potential for enslavement of the person and falsification of precept or truth (1974:242-3).

This strategy is based on the concepts of biblical *absolutism* and cultural relativity, recognizing the Bible, first, as the absolute rule of faith and practice, and following the precept that cultures are to be evaluated in terms of their own values, goals, and worldview assumptions. Thus, through a *biblical cross-cultural perspective*, we are able to look at other people and social groups as having valid alternatives to "our" ways of doing and seeing things. However, the limitation which biblical absolutism places on the application of cultural relativism specifically, and anthropology generally, must always remain as an essential guardian of evangelical missiology.

---

[8] Professional anthropologists take various epistemological positions, some even "anti-relativism"; however, as a corrective to ethnocentrism in missions, Mayers' delineation of biculturalism (closely akin to the position of critical realism) has had a wide impact on missionaries and thus missiological thinking (see Hiebert 1994:21-34, for further discussion).

In addition, among the many practical contributions of cultural anthropology to missiology, has been a method of studying cultural variation as well as culture change through *the distinctions of form and meaning*. Anthropology distinguishes between forms and their meanings. The *forms* of a culture are the observable parts which are material or non-material to which *meanings* are attached by the members of that culture and language. These distinctions made by Ralph Linton (1936:402-4) and incorporated into missiology through the writings of Christian anthropologists (Kraft 1979:64-9; Hiebert 1983:28-9) have become essential to our collection of tools for cross-cultural analysis. As Kraft writes:

> ... *Christianness lies primarily in the functions served and the meanings conveyed by the cultural forms employed*, rather than in the forms themselves. Indeed, at this very point we can most clearly see beyond mere relativism. . . . God seeks to use and to cooperate with human beings in the continued use of relative cultural forms to express absolute supracultural meanings. *The forms of culture are important not for their own sake but for the sake of that which they convey.* And an appropriate fit between form and content is all-important [italics his] (1974:99).

Stephen Grunlan and Marvin Mayers believe this is the "key contribution of anthropology to the theological process" (1988:273). The distinction between cultural forms and meanings is especially important to the development of intercultural theology (ethnotheology). Most Christian anthropologists would agree that the cultural forms in Scripture must be understood in the context of their own culture, and it is their meanings that are sacred, absolute, and authoritative.

The contrasts of form and meaning are understood, for example, in the commandment "do not steal." According to Wayne Dye, this can only mean "do not do those things defined as stealing," and

> even the most literal-minded Christians have an operational interpretation of stealing that is different from what it was in Jesus' day. . . . Jesus

> was in the habit of picking some of the crops and eating them on the spot. This followed ancient Jewish law. . . . If I were to do the same thing in California I could be jailed for theft. Our respective cultures have provided different operational definitions of stealing, though Christians believe the biblical proscription is universally applicable (1985:224-5).

One last contribution, closely related to the previous, should be mentioned as well, though it is doubtless the most controversial: the model of *dynamic equivalence*. Eugene Nida made repeated use of this model in his books and articles dealing with linguistics and cross-cultural communication (see bibliography). Eric North writes:

> As Nida developed and popularized it, dynamic equivalence translation captures the meaning and spirit of the original without being bound to its linguistic structure (formal correspondence). The meaning of the text, the purpose of the original writer, and the relationship of the text to its original cultural setting are guarded as much as possible (quoted in Conn 1984:147-8).

Nida's earliest book, *Customs and Culture* (1954), was based on his lectures to students at SIL and used the model in terms of the anthropological context of communication. Later, in *Message and Mission* (1960), he uses the paradigm of dynamic equivalence to develop techniques of missionary communication. The object of learning here was the cultural context of the *receptor* (R), but also that of the *sender* (S), and the *message* (M). In translation, dynamic equivalence is described as "the closest natural equivalent to the source-language message" and is "directed primarily toward equivalence of response rather than equivalence of form" (Nida 1960:166). There should be a "high degree of equivalence in response or the translation will have failed to accomplish its purpose" (Nida and Taber 1969:24).

Charles Kraft expanded this model in *Christianity and Culture* (1979), in a reexamination of the nature of theologizing across cultures. In the preface of his book, Bernard Ramm wrote, "This is a pioneering effort to synthesize anthropological understanding with theological convictions that are true to the Bible. We have waited too long for such a work . . . " (1979:xi). Perhaps one of the greatest disservices some critics have done Kraft, the author, is to disregard the last sentence in his book: "If you, the reader, find one or more of these concepts unacceptable, you are free to reject it/them without rejecting the remainder of the presentation" (1979:404). What is there here that we **can** agree on as a significant contribution to missiology? How can we carry this model to its next step in our understanding? The issues Kraft brought to our attention have made a profound impact on all who have studied his book. Although Harvie Conn's *Eternal World and Changing World* (1984) has given an excellent critique of the formulations Kraft deals with, these same issues are largely still to be resolved in the field of missiology. Perhaps the next best step would be a revision of his book (1979) including insights from his own thinking since that first edition.

As cross-cultural communicators of an unchanging message, we realize that anthropology has had a significant impact in teaching us that this biblical message must be contextualized in each new culture. This brief outline of some contributions from anthropology will, it is hoped, serve to underline the importance of cooperative efforts in missiology which our fellowship continues to need. In this cause, as an anthropologist, I echo the words of a colleague:

> To bring theology, anthropology, and missions together we must begin with a biblical worldview, one based on the affirmation that Scripture is God's revelation to us. This worldview, particularly as it manifests itself in the New Testament, is the norm whereby we understand and critique all realities. A Christian worldview begins with the reality that God has revealed himself in Scripture, in the person of Jesus Christ, and in the work of the Spirit in the church and the world (Hiebert 1994:11).

## REFERENCE LIST

Barbour, Ian

    1974   *Myths, Models and Paradigms: A Comparative Study in Science and Religion*. New York: Harper and Row.

Bernard, H. Russel

    1994   *Research Methods in Anthropology*. Thousand Oaks, CA: Sage Publications, Inc.

Bodley, John H.

    1994   *Cultural Anthropology: Tribes, States, and the Global System*. Mountain View, CA: Mayfield Publishing Company.

Bohannan, Paul

    1992   *We, The Alien: An Introduction to Cultural Anthropology*. Prospect Heights, IL: Waveland Press, Inc.

Chomsky, N.

    1957   *Syntatic Structures*. The Hague: Mouton.

    1968   *Language and the Mind*. New York: Harcourt, Brace and World.

Conn, Harvie M.

    1984   *Eternal Word and Changing Worlds: Theology, Anthropology, and Mission in Trialogue*. Grand Rapids: Zondervan Publishing House.

    1995   Personal letter. November 6. Chestnut Hill, PA.

Dodd, Carley H.

    1991   *Dynamics of Intercultural Communication*. Dubuque, Iowa: Wm. C. Brown Publishers.

Dye, Wayne T.

    1976   "Toward a Cross-Cultural Definition of Sin." *Missiology* 4 (January): 27-41.

1985 "A Missionary Philosophy of Development." In *Missionaries, Anthropologists, and Culture Change*. Williamsburg, VA: Department of Anthropology, College of William and Mary (pages 215-228).

Ellenberger, John

1995 Personal letter. October 30. Nyack, NY.

Foster, George M.

1965 "Peasant Society and the Image of Limited Good." *American Anthropologist* 67:2 (April): 293-315.

1969 *Applied Anthropology*. Boston: Little, Brown.

Goodenough, Ward H.

1963 *Cooperation in Change*. New York: Russell Sage Foundation.

Goring, Paul

1991 *The Effective Missionary Communicator*. Wheaton: Billy Graham Center.

Grunlan, Stephen A. and Marvin K. Mayers

1988 *Cultural Anthropology: A Christian Perspective*. Grand Rapids: Zondervan (original 1979).

Hall, Edward T.

1959 *The Silent Language*. Garden City, NY: Doubleday.

Haviland, William A.

1993 *Cultural Anthropology*. Fort Worth: Harcourt Brace Jovanovich College Publishers.

Hess, Robert A.

1985 "Perceptions of Medicine and Disease in Nigeria." In *Missionaries and Anthropologists, Part II*. Frank A. Salamone, ed. Williamsburg, VA: Department of Anthropology, College of William and Mary (247-286).

Hesselgrave, David J.

    1991    *Communicating Christ Cross-Culturally*, 2nd ed. Grand Rapids, MI: Zondervan Publishing House.

    1994    *Scripture and Strategy*. Pasadena: William Carey Library.

Hiebert, Paul G.

    1978    "Missions and Anthropology: A Love/Hate Relationship." *Missiology* 6 (April): 165-180.

    1982    "The Flaw of the Excluded Middle." *Missiology* 10 (January): 35-47.

    1983    *Cultural Anthropology*. Reprint from 1976. Grand Rapids: Baker Book House.

    1985    *Anthropological Insights for Missionaries*. Grand Rapids: Baker Books.

    1987    "Critical Contextualization." *Missiology* 12 (July): 287-96.

    1991    "Beyond Anti-Colonialism to Globalism." *Missiology* 19 (July): 263-281.

    1994    *Anthropological Reflections on Missiological Issues*. Grand Rapids: Baker Books.

Keesing, Roger

    1976    *Cultural Anthropology: A Contemporary Perspective*. New York: Holt, Rinehart, and Winston.

Kraft, Charles H.

    1973    "God's Model for Cross-Cultural Communication: The Incarnation." *Evangelical Missions Quarterly* 9:277-84.

    1979    *Christianity In Culture*. Maryknoll, NY: Orbis Books.

    1995    Personal letter. October 30. South Pasadena, CA.

Kottak, Conrad Phillip

    1994    *Cultural Anthropology*. 6th ed. New York: McGraw-Hill, Inc.

Lausanne Committee for World Evangelization
- 1978 The *Willowbank Report*. Wheaton, IL: LCWE.

Linton, Ralph
- 1936 *The Study of Man: An Introduction*. The Century Social Sciences Series. New York: Appleton-Century-Crofts, Inc.

Loewen, Jacob A.
- 1975 *Culture and Human Values*. South Pasadena, CA: William Carey Library.

Luzbetak, Louis J.
- 1993 *The Church and Cultures*. Reprint from 1988. Maryknoll, NY: Orbis Books.

Mayers, Marvin K.
- 1974 *Christianity Confronts Culture*. Grand Rapids: Zondervan Publishing House.
- 1995 Personal letter. November 4. Fort Myers, FL.

McQuilkin, Robertson
- 1992 *Understanding and Applying the Bible*. Chicago: Moody Press.

Nida, Eugene A.
- 1954 *Customs and Cultures: Anthropology for Christian Missions*. New York: Harper and Brothers.
- 1960 *Message and Mission: The Communication of the Christian Faith*. New York: Harper and Row. (Reprinted 1972, Pasadena: William Carey Library).
- 1961 "Christo-Paganism." *Practical Anthropology* 8:1-14.

Nida, Eugene A. and William D. Reyburn
- 1981 *Meaning Across Cultures*. American Society of Missiology Series, No. 4. Maryknoll, NY: Orbis Books.

Nida, Eugene A. and Charles R. Taber
    1969    *The Theory and Practice of Translation.* Leiden: Brill NIV, New International Version of the Bible.

Oberg, Kalvero
    1960    "Culture Shock: Adjustment to New Cultural Environments." *Practical Anthropology* 7:177-182.

Pentecost, Edward C.
    1982    *Issues in Missiology: An Introduction.* Grand Rapids: Baker Book House.
    1995    Personal letter. October. Mabank, TX.

Pike, Kenneth L.
    1954    *Language in Relation to a Unified Theory of the Structure in Human Behavior*, vol. 1. The Hague: Mouton.

Priest, Robert J.
    1994    "Missionary Elenctics: Conscience and Culture." *Missiology* 22 (July): 291-315.

Schrieter, Robert J.
    1991    "Anthropology and Faith: Challenges to Missiology." *Missiology* 19 (July): 283-294.

Smalley, William A., ed.
    1974    *Readings in Missionary Anthropology.* Pasadena: William Carey Library.

Stott, John and Robert T. Coote, eds.
    1979    *Gospel and Culture.* Pasadena: William Carey Library.
    1980    *Down to Earth: Studies in Christianity and Culture.* Grand Rapids: William B. Eerdmans Publishing Co.

Taber, Charles R.
    1978    "The Limits of Indigenization in Theology." *Missiology* 6 (January): 53-79.

Tippett, Alan R.

    1967    *Solomon Islands Christianity*. London: Lutterworth Press.

    1970  *Church Growth and the Word of God*. Grand Rapids: Eerdmans.

    1971  *People Movements in South Polynesia*. Chicago: Moody Press

    1973    *Aspects of Pacific Ethnohistory*. Pasadena: William Carey Library.

    1987    *Introduction to Missiology*. Pasadena: William Carey Library.

Weeks, William H., Paul B. Pedersen and Richard W. Brislin, eds.

    N.d.    *A Manual of Structured Experiences for Cross-Cultural Learning*. Yarmouth, ME: Intercultural Press Inc.

Whiteman, Darrell L., ed.

    1985    *Missionaries, Anthropologists, and Cultural Change*. Studies in Third World Societies, No. 25. Williamsburg, VA: Department of Anthropology, College of William and Mary.

Wilson, Bryan R., ed.

    1970    *Rationality*. New York: Harper and Row.

# 4

# PROTOTYPE SEMANTICS: INSIGHTS FOR INTERCULTURAL COMMUNICATION

## K. A. McElhanon[1]

## SOME CONTEMPORARY ATTITUDES TOWARD THE SOCIAL SCIENCES

The topic for this conference, the social sciences and missiology, is both timeless and timely. It is timeless in that the issues raised by the social sciences in the context of cultural pluralism—precisely the context for missiology as well—have been discussed for more than two millennia.[2] It is timely because there is an uneasiness[3] among some, if not most, evangelical

---

[1] K. A. McElhanon teaches at the University of Texas, Arlington.

[2] See classical dialogues such as that between Plato and Protagoras specifically related to the issue of relativism.

[3] This uneasiness has been called the "Cartesian Anxiety" by Richard Bernstein (1983:19) who says that it is all pervasive and that no area of our lives lies outside its pale. It is the uneasiness felt by all that we are losing our way and may soon be adrift in a sea of ambiguity, that the foundations upon which we have built our society are crumbling. It is "the growing apprehension that there may be nothing—not God, reason, philosophy, science, or poetry—that answers to and satisfies our longing for ultimate constraints, for a stable and reliable rock upon which we can secure our thought and action." Compare Gay's (1993:223-224) Kierkegaardian despair with this Cartesian anxiety: "Kierkegaard perceptively described this kind of refusal to believe that God is able to speak and act in the world in terms of 'despair.' This is the dire condition in which we at-

missiologists and theologians over what they perceive to be an erosion of biblical claims to truth by the soft sciences in general.[4] They are wary, therefore, over the role that the theories, methods, and findings of the social and behavioral sciences are having in the development of missiological theory and practice. My goal is to introduce prototype semantics as a major theoretical advance and to highlight its positive contribution to missiology.

This uneasiness is apparent in the words evangelicals choose when they address the roles of the social sciences vis-à-vis those of theology and missiology. Taber (1991:161) wrote of many missionaries becoming *captive* to cultural anthropology; Hiebert (1993:4) wrote of them becoming *captive* to a modern secular worldview. Rommen (Rommen, et al. 1987:1-3) reported a Norwegian opinion that much of American missiological thought is under the *domination* of the social sciences in contrast to Norwegian missiologists who have Scripture as the only legitimate point of departure. He noted a supposed *abandonment* by German missiologists in the 1920s of a biblical mooring in favor of an applied anthropology and he described German missiological theory as first *embracing* comparative religions, anthropology, ethnology, and geography as supporting disciplines and then later *eschewing* (a stronger word than *shunning* or *avoiding*) the social sciences. He saw valuable lessons in *recognizing the pitfalls* of overemphasizing an anthropological/sociological approach and *becoming alert to potential dangers to avoid repeating the same mistake.*

Later Rommen (1993:1,4) wrote that "the [missiological] enterprise is *adrift on a sea of detheologized paradigms* [and] *awash in competing 'how-to' schemes*" with a :gradual *erosion* of its theological foundation." Guiness (1992:157) wrote of a *lemming-like rush* of church leaders who *forget theology* in the *charge after the latest insights of sociology*—regardless of

---

tempt to define our own existence without reference to or perhaps even over and against God."

[4] The "soft" sciences study human behavior and/or institutions, in which strictly measurable criteria are difficult to obtain so that they rely more on inferences. The "hard" sciences study the natural world, and their hypotheses are more rigorously tested through experimentation and are verified by explicit replication. Also, it may be understood that social science(s) includes behavioral science(s).

where the ideas come from or where they lead to." Drawing a metaphor from contagious diseases, Vanhoozer (1993:24) wrote of theology not being *immune* from the influence of its surrounding culture. This metaphor suggests a quarantine on the behavioral sciences as a way to protect theology, and in that sense resonates with Rommen's use of *eschewing*. My position is that we should not avoid the social sciences, but rather draw upon those sciences when they elaborate upon theological truth. The legitimate findings of the social sciences should be consistent with theological truth. Our challenge is to interpret those findings within a biblical framework.

Richard Bernstein (1983) has identified a number of oppositions which derive from this uneasiness: *objectivism/objectivity* versus *relativism/subjectivity*, *rationality* versus *irrationality*, and *realism* versus *antirealism*. To these one may add from recent missiological literature the following:

1. *scientific* vs. *biblical* (Rommen, et al. 1987:2),
2. *pragmatic* vs. *biblical* concerns in missiology (Rommen 1993:2),
3. *anthropological/sociological* approach vs. *biblical/theological* foundation for mission (Rommen, et al. 1987:2-3; Rommen 1993:3),
4. *social science* base for missions vs. *biblical and theological* base ("Open Letter" 1984:2-3; Rommen, et al. 1987:2-3)
5. *receptor culture* vs. *Scriptures* as controlling the development of theology (Carson 1984:18),
6. *exegeting scripture* vs. *exegeting society* (Rommen, 1993:2),
7. *active theologizing* vs. *applied social science* (Rommen 1993:4),
8. *theologians* vs. *anthropologists* as the best interpreters of Scripture (Hesselgrave 1985:5),
9. *theological paradigms* vs. *how-to-schemes* (Rommen 1993:1),
10. *divine leading and human obedience* vs. *human control* and technique (Hiebert 1993:4),

11. *theology* vs. insights of *modernity and social science* (Rommen 1993:3),
12. *anthropologists* vs. *Christian thinkers* (Taber 1991:171),
13. the *will of God* against the *(cultural) patterns* of this world (Taber 1991:171),
14. *society* [representing the secular behavioral sciences] vs. the *Word of God* in setting the course of world evangelization (Coleman 1993:1),
15. *language* vs. *Scripture* (Carson 1980:20).[5]
16. *pluralist agenda* vs. *truth* (1992:362) [all emphases by K. A. McElhanon].

The use of these contrasts reveals how pervasive and strong is the suspicion on the part of evangelical missiologists and theologians towards the social sciences, particularly towards cultural anthropology. I see a danger in this position solidifying to the extent that missiologists will overlook some truly significant insights gained through a social science perspective.

Linguistics, on the other hand, has been readily accepted. This may be due in large measure to the fact that, as a newly-developing discipline within the social sciences, linguistics assumed a mainly descriptive role. It began with the most accessible features of language: phonetics (Pike 1943), to be followed by intonation (Pike 1945), phonemics (Pike 1947), tone (Pike 1948), then morphology (Nida 1949), and finally grammar and syntax (Pike 1954-60). Linguistic theory was primarily behavioristic, and little attention was paid to rationality in language until the Chomskyan revolution of the 1950s, and even then what was considered rational was so cognitively "deep" that it had little relevance to natural language and language use.

The main significance of linguistics for missiology has been in its appropriation by missionaries for the purposes of

---

[5] He wrote, "[T]he most touted hermeneutical approaches today never enable anyone to hear a sure word from God" in that "they are too closely allied with unacceptable ideological commitments in which the only absolute is language itself."

learning foreign languages (Nida 1957, Larson and Smalley 1972, Brewster and Brewster 1976, D.N. Larson 1984) and, in the case of unwritten languages, in the service of analyzing their phonologies and grammars and providing a methodology for Bible translation (Nida 1947, Nida 1964, Nida and Taber 1969, Beekman and Callow 1974, M.L. Larson 1984). Many will remember that Bible translators borrowed from Transformational Grammar the concept of stripping grammatical transformations from complex sentences in the source language to reduce the text to its simplest "kernel" sentences. Then they transferred the meaning of these kernel sentences to equivalent kernel sentences in the receptor language and added the transformations appropriate for that language (Nida 1964, Nida and Taber 1969). In general linguistics was regarded as a benign discipline, a very useful tool which contributed much to missiology while posing little, if no, threat.

## THE BEGINNINGS OF COGNITIVE LINGUISTICS

Kenneth Pike (1954-1960, Part I:10) extended the phonetic-phonemic distinction of phonological theory to the behavioral domain and coined the terms *emic* and *etic*,[6] the former representing the cultural insiders' understanding of their behavior and how they categorize the world and structure their knowledge of it.[7] The latter represents an outsiders' perspective, that of the analysts as they compare similar events in different cultures. Anthropologists were quick to borrow these terms after the behavioral science revolution, and behavioristic definitions of culture were supplanted by definitions focusing on culture as knowledge.[8] The importance of Pike's suggestion for missiol-

---

[6] See Headland, et al. (1990) for a comprehensive discussion of these terms and their varied senses within an array of social science disciplines.

[7] Spradley (1980:3) cited Malinowski's statement as expressing the goal of ethnography: "to grasp the native's point of view, his relation to life, to realize his vision of his world."

[8] Typical of such definitions is that of Geertz (1973:89): culture is "an historically transmitted pattern of meanings embodied in symbols, a system of inherited conceptions expressed in symbolic forms by means of

ogy cannot be overemphasized, since it is foundational to the goal of missiology, viz., evangelism through faithfully conveying the gospel message to the peoples of other cultures in terms that they will understand.

After culture was redefined as the knowledge one needs to function in the world, a number of researchers from related behavioral science disciplines began to focus their research on understanding how humans conceptualize their world. Among these was the psychologist Eleanor (Heider) Rosch whose studies during the 1970s laid the foundation for the emergence in the 1980s of the discipline of cognitive science, a convergence of the subdisciplines of cognitive psychology, cognitive anthropology, cognitive linguistics, computer science and philosophy. It studies how we experience the world, how we structure our knowledge of that experience, how we store it in short- and long-term memory, and how we retrieve such knowledge to interpret new experiences. It seeks to answer what is unique about human reasoning and what influence culture has upon it. In the remainder of this paper I will focus on the significance of what has been learned about human cognition for missiological theory and method.

## PROTOTYPE SEMANTICS

### Human Cognition According to 1 Cor. 13: 9-11

Prototype semantics is more than just another way to correlate the meanings of sentences with their grammatical forms. In representing a theory about how we interpret our experiences and create new ideas, it gives many insights into what it means for us to have been created in the image of God.

It also gives an account of what is most likely meant by Paul when he used a visual metaphor in 1 Corinthians 13:9 to refer to cognition,[10] that we "see but a poor reflection as in a mir-

---

which men communicate, perpetuate, and develop their knowledge about and attitudes toward life."

[9] For a fuller exegesis of this passage and its relevance to language and revelation, see McElhanon (to appear).

[10] Louw and Nida (1988, 1:383) noted that "the general usage of *ainigma* would seem to point to the meaning of difficulty in understand-

ror" and that we "know in part,"[11] but that after Christ's return we will see him "face-to-face," without the "imperfect medium of human thought and human language" and that we will know "fully."[12] That Paul's focus is on the *quality* rather than on the *quantity* of our knowledge is seen in the contrast between the intervening medium of language, metaphorically pictured as a dim reflection in a mirror on the one hand, and the unimpeded face-to-face encounter on the other. Robertson and Plummer's (1911:299) use of "distorting" to describe the quality of our cognitive processes is too strong in that *distort* indicates a misrepresentation or a false or perverted meaning. Barnes' (1949:254) use of "imperfect" and "indistinct" is much better.[13] We have to keep in mind that God's revelation through human thought and language is fully adequate to accomplish his goals for us.[14]

What this text tells us is that as humans our concepts are at best qualitatively imperfect representations of reality. This innately human quality is not a disadvantage, however, because it still gives us an adequate understanding of how God wants us to respond to his revelation and how we ought to behave toward our fellows. I suggest that this quality of human cognition is best represented by prototype semantics which highlights

---

ing and comprehension rather than in visual perception," so that *blepomen* 'we see' is then interpreted metaphorically as 'we understand.'

[11] Groscheide (1953:309) wrote that the words, "We know in part . . . do not imply that we only know a part of that which is to be known, but rather that the knowing itself is imperfect." For the contrary interpretation that our knowledge is fragmentary see Robertson and Plummer (1911:297) and Morris (1958: 187-88).

[12] Lenski (1937 (1963):568) noted with regard to 1Co 13:12, "The preposition *dia* indicates a medium or a means which intervenes between us and the object of our sight. The fact of the matter is that God himself produced this medium. He descends to us in the Word and speaks about heavenly realities in a human way, for the Word is couched in human expressions. Only in this way can we become cognizant of the heavenly truth."

[13] Barnes (1949:255-56) compared the view in a mirror to that which is face-to-face: "it is like the imperfect view of an object which we have in looking through an obscure and opaque medium compared with the view which we have when we look at it 'face-to-face.'"

[14] Grosheide (1953:311) wrote, "Our vision is not untrue, but it is imperfect as to its degree. When perfection has been reached *then* we shall see *face to face*."

the fact that categories are characterized by central, relatively stable images known as *prototypes*. These prototypes are "conceptual abstractions," and the individual members of any given category exhibit a gradual decline in how well they match that central image. This characteristic allows for the infinite variation that we experience in life, from the most central and normative examples to the most peripheral and bizarre. Such characteristics are considered to be "prototype effects." As I illustrate these prototype effects I will also be describing the theory of prototype semantics. I will begin with vocabulary and then show how the concepts associated with the categorization of vocabulary are paralleled in phonology and grammar.

Prototype effects in vocabulary are easily illustrated by the category *bird*. Picture a kind of bird. What bird came to mind? Americans who live in the northern regions typically picture a robin, perhaps because it is one of the most common birds and one of the first to arrive with spring. Texans generally do not picture a robin because robins visit Texas only for brief periods as they migrate. Rather Texans tend to picture a cardinal. Few people, Texans or otherwise, picture a chicken or a turkey. The fact is that robins are very good examples of a bird, but chickens and turkeys are not. In between are sparrows, crows, starlings, pigeons, quail, pheasant, ducks and geese. These represent a gradation in the membership of the category of *bird*. The idea behind such graded memberships is that people have a concept of "birdness," a conceptual abstraction not identified with any particular bird. I will use the term *prototype* to refer to this conceptual abstraction. This prototype serves as a standard for measuring how well any given example fits. Prototype theory directs our focus toward the more central, best representatives of a category. All non-central examples may be graded according to how well they conform to the prototype, so that as one moves away from the center the examples encountered show increasing deviation. The most bizarre, such as penguins and ostriches, are at the periphery. The boundary itself may be indeterminate; for example, many people have difficulty categorizing the platypus as a bird or an animal.

Prototype effects in grammar may be illustrated by the category *adjective* in English. Huddleston (1984:299-300) noted that the most central adjectives are characterized by four properties: (a) predicate use, e.g., "He was *careless*"; (b) attributive use as the head of an adjective phrase, e.g., "a *careless* mistake"; (c) postpositive use as the head of an adjective phrase, e.g., "people *careless* in their use of money"; and (d) gradable, e.g., "a *most* (or *very*) careless mistake." Only adjectives possess all four of these features, whereas nouns "generally have properties (a) and (b), and to a more limited extent (c) too, but they lack (d)." The importance of this is that nouns and adjectives occur on a continuum so that linguists frequently speak of some forms being more "noun-like" and others being more "adjective-like." The classical categories of discrete and clearly definable nouns, verbs, adjectives, adverbs, etc. have been shown to be idealizations and do not reflect natural language.[15]

Prototype effects in phonology are found in that all sounds may be placed on a continuum with the strongest, most prototypical vowels at one end, and the strongest, most prototypical consonants at the other. For example, from the strongest most sonorant vowel [a], one moves to the weaker vowels [i] and [u], to the semi-vowels [y] and [w], to the less sonorant liquids, [r] and [l], to the more consonantal continuant [β], [δ], [γ], to the stronger voiced stops [b], [d], [g], and then on to the strongest, most consonantal stops, the voiceless, aspirated stops [pʰ], [tʰ], [kʰ]. In this theory the syllable is regarded as having a wave of sonority spread across it, with vowels being the prototypical sonorant sounds and voiceless, short consonants as the most prototypical consonantal sounds.[16]

## Missiological Importance

Kenneth Pike (1954-60) was decades ahead of many of his contemporaries when he suggested that what was needed was a unified theory of language and behavior to account for the continuity between language and behavior. Prototype semantics

---

[15] For prototype effects with regard to English verbs see Bybee and Moder (1983). For the prototypical functions of nouns and verbs in discourse see Hopper and Thompson (1980, 1984), for English adjectives see Thompson (1989) and for noun and pronouns see Sugamoto (1989).

[16] Nathan (1989) provides a sketch of the theory. Decades earlier Pike (1959) observed the wave effect in language when he considered linguistic elements in relation to particles, waves, and fields.

is one such theory, and I will show how it is as applicable to the categories of behavior as it is to those of language.

I have already correlated the blurred imagery of human cognition with the dim images spoken of by Paul in 1 Corinthians 13:9 and have claimed that this is germane to humans having been created in the image of God. Furthermore, I noted that this has to be the case in order for humans to categorize the infinite variety we experience in life. The boundaries of human categories have to be flexible in order for us to adjust our categories to accommodate innovations as well as to deal with all the changes in life.

I also suggest that if human cognition were not characterized by blurred imagery, we would not have a universal gospel which is capable of accommodating all the different ways in which the peoples of diverse cultures structure their knowledge of the world. We know that Jesus' gospel was not compatible with the first century Jewish religious forms. Christ indicated as much by stating that people do not pour new wine (his new and powerful message) into old wineskins (the Jewish religious forms of his day [Mt 9:17]). The truth is that the gospel was intended to be multicultural and to limit its expression to the forms of a single culture would be to fossilize it much like the way in which the Muslim faith has been fossilized in the Islamic cultural forms and the classical Arabic language.[17]

The concept of a prototype as representing the best image of a category with all the members of that category graded from good examples to very marginal examples appears to be applicable to most, if not all, forms of human behavior. For example, people, who dislike someone else's concept and wish to challenge it, do so by constructing the most bizarre examples, those farthest removed from the prototypical norm, and then treating them as though they were the norm. This was a favorite tactic of Jesus' opponents, and it is important to note that Jesus' response was to direct them towards a guiding principle which served as his norm, which in many cases was reinforced with a best example.

Note Matthew's account (19:3-12) of those Pharisees who asked Jesus, "Is it lawful for a man to divorce his wife for any

---

[17] To a Muslim, however, the forms of their faith have been established by divine decree.

and every reason?" It is fair to assume that they were addressing borderline cases "for any and every reason," precisely because the boundaries are indistinct and arguable. In his answer, however, Christ redirected them towards the center, the guiding principle, the standard which serves as the prototype, viz., that God created people as male and female, that in marriage God joined them together, that marriage united them physically, and that marriage was indissoluble. When the Pharisees cited the non-central case of Moses permitting a divorce, Christ again responded on the basis of principle, viz., that Moses did so because their hearts were hardened. In other words, God tolerated non-central cases, but from the beginning the prototypical marriage was meant to be an indissoluble bond between a man and a woman.

On another occasion the Sadducees cited Moses and the practice of levirate marriage, and then proposed what must have been a most bizarre case, that of a woman who had been married to each of seven brothers without bearing any children. They asked him whose wife she would be at the resurrection. Christ was not prepared to argue such borderline cases and directed his response to the more important issue that they didn't know the power of God nor the implication of Moses calling God the God of Abraham, Isaac, and Jacob, viz., that God is the God of the living, for to him all are alive (Lk 20:27-38).[18]

The lesson one could draw from such cases is that it is inappropriate to challenge a concept by suggesting widely deviant, borderline cases and then to treat them as normative. An example from missiology is that of D. A. Carson's (1985) denigration of dynamic equivalence translation with his supposition of a tribe which has had "a long tradition of sacrificing pigs, but has never so much as heard of sheep. Is it in that case justifiable to render John 1:29, 'Look, the swine of God, who

---

[18]Other cases include the Pharisees questioning Christ's aberrant behavior of eating with tax collectors and sinners to which he replied that they should learn what God meant when he said, "I desire mercy, not sacrifice" (Mt 9:11) and John's disciples' question about whether Jesus was "the one who was to come," to which he replied that they should report his basic-level behavior, viz., that he was healing the blind, the lame, the deaf, curing lepers, raising the dead, and preaching the good news to the poor (Mt 9:14). Such behavior was consistent with the character of the "one who was to come."

takes away the sin of the world!'?" Carson wrote that he would argue strongly in the negative and goes on to ask,

> Shall we change *all* such references to "pigs" ("All we like swine have gone astray...")? And if so, do we then make the biblical pig-references clean, and designate some other animal unclean? No; it is surely simpler to preserve "lamb" in the first instance.[19]

His comment seems strange in light of Nida and Taber's (1969:8) statement of a principle of dynamic equivalence: "The translator must attempt to reproduce the meaning of a passage as understood by the writer." In my many years of experience as a Bible translator in Papua New Guinea where there are nearly a thousand linguistic communities practicing swine husbandry, I have heard no one seriously entertain such a substitution.[20] Eugene Nida (personal communication) confirmed that

---

[19] Carson also cited the Sapir-Whorf hypothesis *"in its crudest form*, [which] makes human beings the determined captives of their language," and the New Hermeneutic which, *"in its extreme form*, calls in question the possibility of objective knowledge as text and interpreter progressively 'interpret' one another, without terminus, lost in profound relativity" [emphasis-K.A.M.]. Carson (1980:19) used similar argumentation to challenge opposing schools of hermeneutics "where almost anything—one's presuppositions, one's literary tools, everything one has learned so far (true or false), one's sleep the night before—might be meaningfully labeled 'hermeneutical.'" Also see Carson (1987:217) regarding the new hermeneutic as entailing an "unqualified subjectivity of all knowledge" with every person having a unique "horizon of understanding" unable to communicate with others so that interpreters of texts succumb to a theory that postulates an "unqualified polyvalence of meaning" which leads to a kind of cognitive nihilism. Prototype theory, however, highlights the fact that the majority of the members of society are far from being nihilistic, cognitive or otherwise, and such argumentation that makes use of examples at the periphery is itself marginalized.

[20] For those societies where missionaries have introduced sheep and goats the translators simply use the terms assigned to the animals. In other cases the common practice has been to form a compound from the generic word for "animal" in the vernacular and the foreign word for the animal; thus "animal-sheep" or "animal-goat."

he too had never come across this substitution.[21] Prototype theory draws our attention away from the bizarre examples at the boundaries towards the more normative examples near the center. Responsible translators search for the best examples of a given concept; they do not see how far they can deviate in suggesting borderline examples, and the only scholars I have read suggesting the substitution of a pig for a lamb or sheep have not been translators.[22]

Prototype theory ranks the examples of any category from the more central and typical to the more marginal and atypical. Since the more central examples bear a high correspondence to the prototype and are more predictable, they are also less surprising and less interesting. Life is clearly more exciting at the margins as witnessed by the popularity of most TV talk shows in which major themes such as atypical, alternative life styles or dysfunctional interpersonal relationships abound. So it is with argumentation. Any argument which builds upon examples which are marginal and bizarre by treating them as though they were central and more representative certainly gets our attention, but it is also the weakest because it lacks the authenticity associated with arguments based upon the central and more normative examples. Prototype theory draws our attention away from the margins toward the center, and therefore it militates against all inclinations toward deviance.

---

[21] When Carson (1993:43) repeated the example, he wrote, "this illustration is probably overdrawn" and that "it is so extreme that few translators would opt for the pigs."

[22] Another is Hesselgrave (1985:5) who depicted what he regarded as a "sub-orthodox" view of contextualizing the biblical message by supposing that if "the people in an Indonesian culture highly prize pigs and use them in their sacrifices and John intended to convey a positive appreciation of Jesus when he introduced Him as the Lamb of God (Jn 1:29) in first century Jewish culture, then gospel communication may be better served by the pig analogy than by the lamb analogy. . . . In fact, entire passages of Scripture may require similar revision."

## THE PERCEIVED WORLD STRUCTURE

The world is amazingly complex, filled with an infinite number of attributes.[23] The classical view treated these attributes as though they were essentially random and chaotic, and that any order and structure that they exhibited was imposed upon them by the humans who perceived them.[24] If such were the case then all of our knowledge would be culturally determined and relative.

The fact is, however, that we do not perceive the world as a disarray of unstructured attributes. Rather, we recognize that objects in the world are characterized by what Rosch (1978:29) has called a "high correlational structure," i.e., they have attributes which normally occur together in clusters. Rosch (1977:27) noted the attributes which are characteristic of birds did not just happen to occur together and constitute birds.[25] Creatures that have feathers are more likely to have wings than are creatures that have fur. Rosch calls this the principle of "perceived world structure." What this principle accounts for is that the presence of one attribute implies the presence of one or more others.

---

[23] D'Andrade (1981:180) has commented briefly with regard to the amount of data confronting us, if it were perceived as chaotic and unorganized. "No one knows how large is the size of the corpus of information represented by any given culture. Perhaps it is not too grandiose to suggest that the number of bits or units of information is comparable to the number of stars in the universe or the grains of sand in the sea. Conjectures on how much any one "typical" adult knows range from "several hundred thousand to several million" and that "the total informational pool carried by the entire population for a society might be something like a hundred to ten thousand times the amount that any one person knows, yielding estimates of the total cultural information pool ranging from a few million to ten billion chunks of information."

[24] Rosch (1973, 1975) traces this model back to Aristotle.

[25] This observation should have something to say about the plausibility of the theory of evolution. If we reject the notion that attributes do not occur together then it seems reasonable to say that evolution is somehow goal directed. But evolution is not generally thought of as having a goal, but rather being a response to external pressures.

## Missiological Importance

The importance this principle has for missiology is that any concept we wish to transfer to another culture has its own unique complex of associations. Moreover, the concept does not enter a vacuum in the other culture, for there are very few, if any, entities which are totally autonomous. Most likely the concept to be transferred has to fit into some existing category in a world already highly structured with quite different associations.

As a result, two notions have to be implemented with greater caution. First, one has to be careful in transferring a concept by translating its term by the closest equivalent in the receptor language. An example from Papua New Guinea concerns the substitution of a gourd for the wineskins into which wine was stored for fermentation (Mt. 9:17). The translator chose to substitute a local gourd which was traditionally hollowed out, dried, and used for storage. The gourd, however, was traditionally used to store betelnut, never used for storing a liquid. The translation of the verse was certainly true—"Neither do people pour fresh grape juice into old gourds"—simply because no one had ever done it nor was likely to. But the translation had no relevance to the meaning Christ sought to convey by his illustration.

Second, and more serious, is the concept that one can "Christianize" vocabulary which has pagan meaning. This same translator chose the vernacular word for *white magic* to express the biblical concept of *blessing* (McElhanon 1969). The only similarity was that both were associated with benefits. However, not only are the associations with white magic unacceptable, but also to associate Jesus with the performance of white magic entails that he was a shaman, and that he had power because he knew the correct ritual for producing results. It is no wonder that the area of Papua New Guinea where this translation has been used is one of the centers of cargo ideology—the belief that Europeans obtain their wealth from God, usually with the aid of their ancestors. The translation of the New Testament contributed much to its development.

## THE BASIC LEVEL

**An Overview**

We subcategorize the category *animal* according to *dogs, cats, rats, horses, cows,* etc. Each of these subcategories are further subcategorized; e.g., we subcategorize *dogs* as to whether they are *poodles, terriers, spaniels, hounds,* etc. This kind of categorization results in a taxonomy. What is significant is that a taxonomy is regarded as having one level which is more "basic" than the others. This "basic level" is the most abstract level at which humans can form images of specific objects or entities (Rosch, et al. 1976, Rosch 1978). For example, we can form an image of a *dog,* but not of an *animal. Dog,* as a basic-level entity, has many more features than does its superordinate term, *animal,* and the features are more salient, i.e., they come to mind more readily. When asked to describe a *dog,* we can rather quickly list such features as that it barks, is very affectionate, wags its tail, responds to human emotions and appears to exhibit emotions of its own. A request for a description of *animal,* however, requires much more considered thought. This is because when we interact with a *dog* we don't think of it as interacting with an *animal.* We interact with its basic-level characteristics. The characteristics of *animal,* such as that it is alive, warm blooded, air-breathing, etc., are not characteristic only of dogs and so do not come to mind as readily when we think of *dog.*

In comparison to the entities at the basic level, those at its subordinate level, such as the breeds of dogs, also involve significant numbers of features, but many of those features are basic-level features which are carried down to the subordinate level. Most of the ways in which humans interact with dogs can also be said of most breeds of dogs. The ways that we feed dogs, groom them, play with them, and show them affection are largely uniform, with specific physical features such as the size of the dog or the quantity of its hair having little impact on our interactions. Of course some breeds, such as the huge St. Bernard, the petite Chihuahua, and the hairless Chinese Crested require us to modify our interactions, but these breeds are atypical and the modifications insignificant.

That our interaction with basic-level entities is largely uniform is further shown by the ways in which we interact with items of furniture. The activity of sitting in a chair is basically the same whether it is soft-cushioned or wooden; that of reclining is basically the same action for all beds, whether we lie on mattresses or water bladders, and it does not change much for cribs, stretchers, and even hammocks. There is, however, no uniform way to interact with the more abstract, superordinate concept of *furniture*.

Table A presents some terms of basic-level entities and the superordinate categories to which they belong. What has been said about *dog* and *animal* is true of the other sets as well. If we are asked to picture a *tool*, the best we can do is to picture a representative tool from the basic level, e.g., a *hammer*, *chisel*, *saw*, etc. We simply find it impossible to picture the more abstract concept of *tool*. Furthermore, there is also no uniform way for us to interact with a *tool*, but our actions with a *screw driver*, regardless of whether it is designed for slotted or Phillips screws, is basically the same. So also our use of a saw, whether it is a handsaw or a hacksaw.

| SUPER-ORDINATE LEVEL | animal | tool | musical instrument | motor vehicle | furniture |
|---|---|---|---|---|---|
| **BASIC LEVEL** | dog | hammer | guitar | car | chair |
| | cat | chisel | piano | bus | bed |
| | rat | saw | organ | train | couch |
| | horse | wrench | flute | truck | table |
| | cow | drill | trumpet | | dresser |

TABLE A: Basic-level Objects.

The fact that the basic level is the most abstract level at which we can picture entities and interact with them entails that it is also the level at which we live out our lives, the level of daily activity. If we live our lives at the basic level, it is probable that the more abstract concepts at the superordinate level are those which motivate our basic-level activities; it is at the superordinate level that we locate our values. For the purposes of our discussion it is more important to recognize the distinction between the basic and superordinate levels than it is to try to determine how many levels there are above the basic level and what sort of conceptual distance separates them.

The relationship of the more abstract concepts at the superordinate level to our activities at the basic level can be illustrated by what Paul wrote in Philippians 4.8, "Finally, brothers, whatever reflects *integrity*, whatever is *virtuous*, whatever is *proper*, whatever is *faultless*, whatever is *pleasing*, whatever is *admirable*—if anything is *excellent* or *praiseworthy*—think about such things."[26] What Paul provides is a list of abstract concepts which can only be realized by behavior expressed at the basic level, i.e., by the "whatevers," which are consistent with each abstract quality. Paul gives the command to be focused on those forms of behavior which exemplify the qualities he has enumerated.

The concept that the behavior at the basic level needs to be consistent with the superordinate, abstract qualities is reflected in Paul's observation (Ro 14.13-19) that the Roman Christians could serve Christ, please God, and achieve the approval of non-Christians by not insisting on the basic-level activity of eating meat. To eat meat would upset their fellow Christians and not be an expression of the superordinate concept of love. It would not be in character with the behavior of those who submitted to God's authority. It would not be proper and would not result in peace and joy in the Holy Spirit.

This concept is also consistent with Christ's answer to John when John wanted to baptize him, "Let it be so now, it is proper for us to do this to fulfill all righteousness" (Mt 3:15). Thus *righteousness*, as the more abstract concept, is expressed by a basic-level activity, in this case, the act of baptism. There are other proper ways to fulfill righteousness, and also some that are improper. Table B displays these as well as some examples of wickedness.

---

[26]My translation of the key words is based upon Louw and Nida (1988).

| | righteousness | | wickedness |
|---|---|---|---|
| **SUPERORDINATE LEVEL** | | | |
| | (proper expressions) | (improper expressions) | |
| **BASIC LEVEL** | act of baptism (Mt 3.15) | break and teach others to break the law (Mt 5.19-20) | hit on cheek (Mt 5.39) |
| | give to meet the needs of the poor (Mt 6.3) | give to receive from those who watch (Mt. 6.2) | sue for tunic (Mt 5.40) |
| | private prayer to address God (Mt 6.6) | | buy the power of the Holy Spirit (Acts 8.19-22) |
| | meaningful prayer (Mt 6.8-13) | public prayer to gain attention (Mt 6.5) | betray someone (Jn 19.11) |
| | discrete fasting (Mt 6.17-18) | meaningless prayer (Mt 6.7) | imprison debtor (Mt 18.23-35) |
| | give cold water (Mt. 10.42) | obvious fasting to gain attention (Mt 6.16) | kill land owner's servants and son (Mt 21.33-41) |
| | | | not using one's capabilities (Mt 25.14-30) |
| | | | filthy living (2 Pet 2.7) |

TABLE B: Righteousness and Wickedness

In a sense Table B merges the concept of prototype with that of the basic and superordinate levels. We saw how the basic-level category of *bird* exhibits prototype effects when particular kinds of birds are graded according to how well they match our concept of birdness. The same is true of the basic-level expressions of the more abstract concepts at the superordinate level; e.g., the various expressions of righteousness or wickedness may be graded according to how well they conform to the corresponding prototype given at the superordinate level. Christ said as much when he replied to Pilate, "The one who betrayed me is guilty of a greater sin" (Jn 19:11). This is possibly due to the fact that betrayal is regarded as a greater breach of the concept of commitment than are acts of minor physical violence or that of litigation. The implication here is that sin is basically a relational concept—a breach in relationship, alienation.

## Missiological Importance

What is important for us who are in intercultural evangelism to recognize is that primacy should be given to those more abstract concepts at the superordinate level such as love, submission, kindness, patience, and honesty. It is these concepts that are most likely to have universal applicability. How these concepts are expressed at the basic level, however, is likely to differ across cultures and also to change within our own culture. For example, theft as a superordinate concept is universal, but the kinds of things that qualify as capable of being stolen and the conditions which define when theft occurs differ from culture to culture. In some non-technological cultures it may be that fire is categorized along with water and air as something that belongs to everybody. One cannot regard it as personal property and deprive others of it. To do so would be inhumane, but to take it would be to take what one is entitled to. Just because Western technology enables people to capture fire, put it on the end of a stick and sell it does not change the category to which it belongs in such societies. Therefore, to judge as thieves those who help themselves to matches is to impose our categories upon them. And the one who withholds matches may be perceived by them as behaving selfishly. One is well advised to recognize that thievery, as a violation of someone else's welfare, violates the mutual commitment that God expects to be normative for his people, and to realize that there are dangers in focusing on particular acts that constitute thievery in one culture while overlooking the underlying principle. Anyone who confuses the forms of behavior at the basic level with the principles of the superordinate level are in danger of forcing cultural forms on another people and having them confuse those forms with the gospel truth.

# CONCLUDING REMARKS

The attitude of many evangelical theologians and missiologists toward the social sciences may be characterized by hypervigilance and fear, hypervigilance that the theoretical bases for the social sciences may be pernicious to the theological/missiological endeavors, and fear that those who utilize the social sciences will abandon biblical theology.

In 1981 Mansell Pattison made an observation which is still timely today:

> If behavioral science has ignored a normative Christian theology, so too has the Church ignored the profound implications of behavioral science. If the Church does not speak meaningfully to the behavioral science enterprise, then the Church has not listened attentively to what the behavioral scientists are saying. There is a common ground and a common cause, but there is no common dialogue. This is the agenda before us (1981:421).

It is time to set aside old fears and take a fresh look at the social sciences, since theology and missiology address the same domain. Truth is singular and exhibits a coherence. We will do well not to ignore the insights of the social sciences but rather to build upon those which are consistent with biblical truth and thereby gain a richer perspective on what it means to be humans and how we as humans are to live together in harmony in an increasingly shrinking community.

## REFERENCE LIST

"Open Letter to Future Missionaries"
    1984    *Trinity World Forum* 10:1 (Fall): 2-3.

Barnes, Albert
    1949    *First Corinthians. Notes on the New Testament: Explanatory and Practical*. Grand Rapids, MI: Baker.

Beekman, John, and John Callow
    1974    *Translating the Word of God*. Grand Rapids, MI: Zondervan.

Bernstein, Richard J.

    1983    *Beyond Objectivism and Relativism: Science, Hermeneutics, and Praxis.* Philadelphia: University of Philadelphia Press.

Brewster, Tom and Betty Sue Brewster

    1976    *Language Acquisition Made Practical: Field Methods for Language Learners.* Colorado Springs, CO: Lingua House.

Bybee, Joan and Carol Moder

    1983    "Morphological Classes as Natural Categories." *Language* 59: 251-270.

Carson, D. A.

    1980    "Hermeneutics: A brief assessment of some recent trends." *Themelios* 5(2): 12-20.

    1984    "A Sketch of the Factors Determining Current Hermeneutical Debate in Cross-Cultural Contexts." In *Biblical Interpretation and the Church: The Problem of Contextualization.* Nashville: Thomas Nelson. Pp. 11-29.

    1985    "The Limits of Dynamic Equivalence in Bible Translation." *Evangelical Review of Theology* 9(3).

    1987    "Church and Mission: Reflections on Contextualization and the Third Horizon." In *The Church in the Bible and the World.* D. A. Carson, ed. Grand Rapids, MI: Baker; Exeter: Paternoster.

    1993    "New Bible Translations: An Assessment and Prospect." In *The Bible in the Twenty-first Century.* Howard Clark Kee, ed. New York: American Bible Society. Pp. 37-67.

Coleman, Robert E.

    1993    "A Word from the Editor." *TWF* 19(1, Fall 1993): 1.

Corrigan, Roberta, Fred Eckman and Michael Noonan, eds.

    1989    *Linguistic Categorization.* Amsterdam and Philadelphia: John Benjamins.

D'Andrade, Roy G.

    1981    "The Cultural Part of Cognition." *Cognitive Science* 5: 179-195.

Gay, Craig M.

    1993    "Plurality, Ambiguity, and Despair in Contemporary Theology." *JETS* 36(2): 209-227.

Geertz, Clifford

    1973    *The Interpretation of Cultures.* New York: Basic Books.

Groscheide, F. W.

    1953    *Commentary on the First Epistle to the Corinthians.* The New International Commentary on the New Testament. Grand Rapids, MI: Eerdmans.

Guiness, Os

    1992    "Sounding Out the Idols of Church Growth." In *No God but God.* Os Guiness and John Seel, eds. Chicago: Moody Press.

Headland, Thomas N., Kenneth L. Pike, and Marvin Harris, eds.

    1990    *Emics and Etics: The Insider/Outsider Debate.* Newbury Park, CA, London, and New Delhi: Sage Publications.

Hesselgrave, David J.

    1985    "Evangelism and the Contextualization of the Gospel." *TWF* 10(2): 4,5,8.

Hiebert, Paul G.

    1993    "De-theologizing Missiology: A Response." *TWF* 19 (1): 4.

Hopper, Paul and Sandra Thompson

>   1980    "Transitivity in Grammar and Discourse." *Language* 56: 251-299.
>
>   1984    "The Discourse Basis for Lexical Categories in Universal Grammar." *Language* 60: 703-752.

Huddleston, Rodney

>   1984    *Introduction to the Grammar of English*. Cambridge: Cambridge University Press.

Larson, Donald N.

>   1984    *Guidelines for Barefoot Language Learning: An Approach through Involvement and Independence*. St. Paul, MN: CMS, Pub.

_____, and William A. Smalley

>   1972    *Becoming Bilingual: A Guide to Language Learning*. South Pasadena, CA: William Carey Library (1984); Lanham, MD: University Press of America.

Larson, Mildred L.

>   1984    *Meaning-based Translation: A Guide to Cross-language Equivalence*. Lanham, MD: University Press of America.

Lenski, R. C. H.

>   (1937) 1963    *The Interpretation of St. Paul's First and Second Epistles to the Corinthians*. Minneapolis: Augsburg.

Louw, Johannes P., and Eugene A. Nida, eds.

>   1988    *Greek-English Lexicon of the New Testament Based on Semantic Domains*. 2 vols. New York: United Bible Societies.

McElhanon, K. A.

>   1969    "Current Cargo Beliefs in the Kabwum Sub-District." *Oceania* 39(3): 174-186.

McElhanon, K. A.

(to appear) *1 Corinthians 13.9-11: Reflections on a Glass Darkly.*

McGrath, Alister E.

    1992    "The Challenge of Pluralism for the Contemporary Christian Church." *JETS* 35(3): 361-373.

Morris, Leon

    1958    *The First Epistle of Paul to the Corinthians: An Introduction* and *Commentary.* The Tyndale New Testament Commentaries. Grand Rapids, MI: Eerdmans.

Nathan, Geoffrey S.

    1989    "Preliminaries to a Theory of Phonological Substance: The Substance of Sonority." In *Linguistic Categorization.* Roberta Corrigan, Fred Eckman and Michael Noonan, eds. Amsterdam and Philadelphia: John Benjamins. Pp. 55-67.

Nida, Eugene A.

    1947    *Bible Translating: An Analysis of Principles and Procedures with Special Reference to Aboriginal Languages.* New York: American Bible Society.

    1949    *Morphology: The Descriptive Analysis of Words.* Ann Arbor, MI: University of Michigan Press.

    1957    *Learning a Foreign Language: A Handbook Prepared Especially for Missionaries.* New York: Friendship Press.

    1964    *Toward a Science of Translation.* Leiden: E. J. Brill.

    1975    *Exploring Semantic Structures.* München: Wilhelm Fink Verlag.

_____ and Charles R. Taber

    1969    *The Theory and Practice of Translation.* Leiden, Netherlands: E. J. Brill.

Pattison, E. Mansell

1981 "The Behavioral Sciences in a Christian Perspective." *Anglican Theological Review* 63(4): 405-421.

Pike, Kenneth L.

1943 *Phonetics: A Critical Analysis of Phonetic Theory and a Technic for the Practical Description of Sounds.* Ann Arbor, MI: University of Michigan Press.

1945 *The Intonation of American English.* Ann Arbor, MI: University of Michigan Press.

1947 *Phonemics: A Technique for Reducing Languages to Writing.* Ann Arbor, MI: University of Michigan Press

1948 *Tone Languages.* Ann Arbor, MI: University of Michigan Press

1954-1960 *Language in Relation to a Unified Theory of the Structure of Human Behavior.* 3 parts. Preliminary edition. Glendale, CA: Summer Institute of Linguistics (Revised in Pike (1967)).

1959 "Language as Particle, Wave, and Field." *The Texas Quarterly* 2: 37-54. Reprinted: 1972. *Kenneth L. Pike: Selected Writings.* Pp. 129-143.

1967 *Language in Relation to a Unified Theory of the Structure of Human Behavior.* Second, revised edition. The Hague: Mouton.

Robertson, Archibald, and Alfred Plummer

1911 *A Critical and Exegetical Commentary on the First Epistle of St. Paul to the Corinthians.* International Critical Commentary. New York: Charles Scribner's Sons.

Rommen, Edward

1993 "The De-Theologizing of Missiology." *TWF*, 19(1): 1-4.

_____, David Hesselgrave, and John McIntosh

    1987    "American Missiology—Which Way." *Trinity World Forum* 12 (2, Winter 1987): 1-3.

Rosch, Eleanor H.

    1973    "Natural Categories." *Cognitive Psychology* 4: 328-350.

    1975    "Universals and Cultural Specifics in Human Categorization." In *Cross-cultural Perspectives on Learning*. Richard W. Brislin, Stephen Bochner, and Walter J. Lonner, eds. New York: John Wiley & Sons. Pp. 177-206.

    1977    "Human Categorization." In *Studies in Cross-cultural Psychology*, Vol. 1. Neil Warren, ed. London, New York, and San Francisco: Academic Press. Pp. 3-49.

    1978    "Principles of Categorization." In *Cognition and Categorization*. Eleanor Rosch and Barbara B. Lloyd, eds. New York: John Wiley. Pp. 27-48.

_____, Carolyn B. Mervis, Wayne D. Gray, David M. Johnson, and Penny Boyes-Braem

    1976    "Basic Objects in Natural Categories." *Cognitive Psychology* 8: 382-439.

Spradley, James P.

    1980    *Participant Observation*. Orlando: Harcourt Brace Jovanovich.

Sugamoto, Nobuko

    1989    "Pronominality: A Noun-pronoun Continuum." In Corrigan, et al. Pp. 267-291.

Taber, Charles R.

    1991    *The World Is Too Much with Us: "Culture" in Modern Protestant Missions*. Macon, GA: Mercer University Press.

Thompson, Sandra A.

1989 "A Discourse Approach to the Cross-linguistic Category 'Adjective.'" In Corrigan et al. Pp. 245-265.

Vanhoozer, Kevin J.

1993 "The World Well Staged? Theology, Culture, and Hermeneutics." In *God and Culture: Essays in Honor of Carl F. H. Henry.* D. A. Carson and John D. Woodbridge, eds. Grand Rapids, MI: Eerdmans; Carlisle, England: Paternoster. Pp. 1-30.

# 5

# PSYCHOLOGY AND MISSIONS: A HISTORY OF MEMBERCARE IN CROSS-CULTURAL MINISTRY

### Brent Lindquist[1]

## BACKGROUND TO PSYCHOLOGY AND MISSIONS

Psychology seems to be a difficult concept to manage in some parts of the Christian church. Paying too much attention to psychological principles invariably causes one to be viewed as not being "Christian" or spiritual enough. Paying too little attention seems to have similar problematic effects at the other end of the spectrum. The history of psychology in missions is similar (Hunter and Mayers 1987:269-273). This paper[2] may struggle from similar critique, by trying to walk down a center path.

---

[1] Brent Lindquist is a licensed psychologist, and is the president and clinical director of Link Care Center.

[2] This paper is a shortened version of a longer work on the history of psychology and missions, being written in honor of the thirtieth anniversary of Link Care Center. The author is indebted to many people who have provided input and guidance. They include, but are not limited to: John Powell, Kelly O'Donnell, and Tom Ekblad. It has been a privilege to have worked with all the Link Care staff over the last twenty years. Their encouragement and support has and continues to be greatly appreciated. Two in particular have been major mentors: Stan Lindquist, who has been like Barnabas, and Don Larson, who has been like Paul. Finally, special recognition goes to Joy Bustrum. Joy was the Summer 1995 Extern at Link Care, as part of her education at Biola University. She provided valuable research assistance.

Psychological dimensions of life and personality styles have been evident from the very beginning in missionary efforts. One can look at the experience of Paul in his encouragement of Timothy and his discouragement with John Mark; his involvement with Silas and Barnabas, and the disagreements which arose out of those relationships. The letter to Philemon is one example of many of Paul's attempts to deal with a psychological component within the context of spiritual growth and development. (One can also see social work principles at work in attempting to care for the widows of Jerusalem.)

The more recent missionary endeavors of the last two hundred years show many examples of pronounced psychological disturbance on the part of our early missionary forebears (Tucker and Andrews 1992). In brief, David Brainerd in the 1700s suffered depression and loneliness, and Dorothy Carey's increasingly well-known story of mental breakdown in India are but the earliest examples of the involvement of psychological issues or symptoms in the life of the missionary (Beck 1993:9-17). In the 1800s there were sex scandals and alcoholism problems apparent in the South Sea islands. A. B. Simpson evidently had periods of depression. Adoniram Judson, responded to his wife's and daughter's deaths with a mental disorder and recovery. J. Hudson Taylor exhibited depression and related difficulties. Mary Morrison (1800s) struggled with adjustment, depression and mental breakdown, and Mary Livingston was sent back to England alone with her children where the church ignored her and she struggled with alcoholism and depression.

In this century, efforts began after World War II to develop a more psychological response to the development of such symptoms in missionaries. It probably could be argued that this arose out of a general cultural response to the impact of World War II, in particular, on our culture. The concepts of shell shock, which probably developed into post-traumatic stress disorder in the present time, caused people to wonder about the impact of significant change through surviving the trauma of war or being damaged by the trauma of war and the need for additional care in response to cross-cultural ministry.

## PRESENT DEVELOPMENT OF PSYCHOLOGY AND MISSIONS

In the late 1950s and early 1960s at least three events happened which pointed to a growing awareness and development of the behavioral sciences and psychology in the whole area of missions. First, Marvin Mayers, of Wycliffe Bible Translators, gave an address to the EFMA/IFMA agencies on behavioral sciences in missions. Although his approach looked more at anthropology than psychology, at least it pointed out the necessity of understanding these other disciplines. At the same time, Clyde Narramore wrote a book on the needs and problems of overseas missionaries, which was the result of a long trip to the mission field right after the Narramore Foundation was established (Powell 1995).

Finally, around the same time Stanley Lindquist was on sabbatical from the then Fresno State College working on a book. But he was also visiting missionaries throughout Europe and living with them for a few days at a time with his family. As a psychologist he began to apply some of what he knew to help missionaries address the problems of daily living, cultural stress and the other developmental issues which many of them had been experiencing. This experience and subsequent vision resulted in the establishment of Link Care Center on December 31, 1964. Additionally, the counseling department at Wycliffe was started by Phil Grossman about this time. The early 1960s evidently was something of a germinal period in which some of these ideas emerged among a few widely diverse people, sometimes working with little knowledge of the others. Over three decades it has grown into the more cooperative effort that we see today.

## PSYCHOLOGY, OR MEMBERCARE

It is difficult to discuss the influence of psychology in missions by working from the discipline of psychology alone. A popular word that people in missions with mental-health leanings are using is the word "Membercare." Psychology as a discipline concerns itself with an application of scientific or empirically derived knowledge from that discipline to concerns such as missions. These include psychological testing, knowledge of human behavior and personality styles, applications of understandings regarding conflict resolution or management, stress management, and the application of the understanding of mental disorders and psychopathology to the missionary endeavor. Membercare, as it is becoming increasingly defined (O'Donnell 1988), is a multi-disciplinary field or movement focusing on the mission and its structure, its policy, its relationships, and its people in ways that facilitate personal and professional growth. What was once the more exclusive domain of the psychologist has increasingly become shared with the pastoral counselor and, to a lesser extent, with various human resource personnel (Dennett 1990, Hesselgrave 1983, O'Donnell 1986, O'Donnell 1987, Ritchey and Rosik, 1993).

In the "modern" age of psychology and missions, or membercare and missions, there are a number of people who have shown significant leadership. Since 1980 John Powell and David Wickstrom, two psychologists in private practice and university work, have been hosting a "Mental Health and Missions Conference" for a small group of people interested in crossing the cultural boundaries of their disciplines and learning from each other. These events are continuing, and have been quite stimulating for all the parties involved. In addition, John Powell has served overseas regularly as a consultant on psychological issues with various mission organizations.

Link Care Center, since its inception years ago, has continued to grow, develop and respond to a broader multi-disciplinary perspective in its application of psychological principles to the missionary lifespan. Donald N. Larson, Ph.D., linguist and anthropologist, joined the staff on a consultant basis in 1982 and on a more regular basis in 1988. Since that time Link Care has been working, particularly in its language acquisition prefield orientation programs, to present a more multi-perspectival approach, focusing on the disciplines of psychology, anthropology, linguistics, and sociology. This arose out of the concern of both Larson and Lindquist that in order to be effective, missionaries needed to have a good understanding of the inter-relatedness of their linguistic, cultural and psychological makeups. To a lesser extent, this has been occurring in the counseling aspect of Link Care, but this work is still going on.

Over the years numerous other people have been working, either mostly within certain missions or with smaller groups of missions, being resource people for assessment, for counseling, and for care. It is useful to note agencies like Barnabas International, which focused initially on pastoral care and conferences; Interaction, which has focused extensively on the needs of the missionary children; Narramore Christian Foundation, which has had a long running program on missionary kid re-entry; and Missionary Internship, an older organization like Link Care, which has focused more on application of psychological principles to prefield orientation. Even more recently, there have arisen networks of organizations that are interested in providing rest and recreation services to missionary families, pastoral counseling, and psychological care. The Caregivers Forum is a network of over fifty such entities which meets regularly and tries to network and fellowship together in order to better understand the needs of the people that the Forum members serve.

## THE FUTURE OF PSYCHOLOGY AND MISSIONS

In one sense, psychology can rest easy. There will always be a place for psychological resources within the missions context. The stress and strain of working where one doesn't belong will continue to produce stress and casualties. This could be construed as a rather fatalistic presupposition, but a survey of any of the vocations that occur in high stress or traumatic conditions reveals that there is always a stress and casualty factor (Carr 1994). Besides striving to prevent all casualties, it makes more sense to address the environments that produce casualties. By understanding the environment it is possible to better aid the people who will be working there and offer focused training and remediation.

Certainly, a major area in which psychology can continue to assist missions is in the whole area of screening and assessment. There are presently two major schools of thought regarding screening and assessment. One school would assert that it is better to screen out people with the use of psychological criteria that are likely to cause problems in the missionary environment. Another school would use the psychological assessment criteria to understand the people as well as possible in order to aid them in getting the training and experience they need to be the most effective people they can be in a cross-cultural environment. Both approaches have their pros and cons.

Attempting to screen out all possible problem areas may mean that one will screen out those who who would later prove to be effective missionaries. On the other hand, screening only to understand people better may allow those who shouldn't be in cross-cultural ministry to continue on that path when it might have been more charitable to them, their families, and those they serve if they had remained at home. Hopefully, a balance will continue to be developed which utilizes the best of both streams in understanding and evaluating.

The major danger to psychology, from the author's perspective, is in not recognizing that it is inherently an ethnocentric body of knowledge more dependent on North American cultural values and mores in its entirety than it readily believes (Hesselgrave 1987). Even to the present, most training programs focus on the individual and intra-psychic issues when the world functions more on a systemic—as in family or community/tribe—model with inter-psychic issues prominent as well. Traditional treatment often focuses on the individual, then the couple or the family, and ignores the larger organizational community network in which behavior exists. Finally, many treatment models are inherently expensive in terms of time and finances. Finances are an area that is increasingly becoming strained as missions seek to adjust to the new millennium and the giving realities of the younger generation.

Those of us in North America also need to recognize that the North American missionary population is marching toward minority status sooner than we realize. Continuing to extol or utilize in a major way treatment techniques, concepts or philosophies that are more North American than they are cross-cultural will have potentially troublesome consequences. Not the least of these is making the North American mental health professional increasingly marginalized in the larger global, missionary and church endeavors.

To continue to be an active force in the larger missionary endeavor it may be that psychology should refocus back on two of its traditional strengths—assessment and research—and focus on providing ways to determine if new strategies of managing people and dealing with them are actually effective.

Membercare, as it is envisioned, is more of a conglomeration and tends to have a very pragmatic as opposed to scientific base of approach. Much of this is encouraging because it seems that mission organizations are really trying to find ways of taking better care of their people. However, some of the strategies of care may not be as efficient or effective as they should be. Psychological research methods may be able to help with these kinds of issues.

A new paradigm needs to be investigated. Many of the psychologists involved in missions are clinicians. Their focus is on the identification and treatment of varyous conditions from psychopathology to problems in living. Rather than focusing on the end result of dealing with problems, psychology could make a shift and focus on identifying what it is that makes people effective. There would need to be an additional shift in terms of gathering more information from the important disciplines of linguistics, anthropology, and sociology—to name just three—in order to understand what makes a person effective in places where they don't belong.

Coming at the problem from the perspective of the desired end (that is, from the effective missionary end and identifying what some of the critical issues, characteristics or traits are and then developing screening processes, assessment processes, or remediative processes to help people get at those characteristics that may be dormant, or even non-existent in themselves) can be a very appropriate way for psychology to get out of its illness-oriented frame of reference, and to be seen by the larger church community as a valuable resource. Identifying what it is that makes somebody want to change their way of life in response to a relationship with someone else and what it is in the characteristics of that outside relationship that facilitates this could be very beneficial. Certainly, this is not talking about the spiritual attributes, but more of the relational and behavioral attributes and communication strategies. This is not to discount the Holy Spirit, but simply to ask how we can use psychology to help us in understanding some of the ways in which we behave as human beings so as to facilitate the working of the Holy Spirit. There appears to be too much adversity between psychology and the church. Unfortunately, this has prevented the consideration of sound psychological principles in he missions context. Indeed, even considering the discipline of psychology as opposed to biblical values has set up unnecessary dichotomies. Seeing psychology as a threat to missions and the church prevents the church from benefitting from some important insights—as well as some important care that can be provided.

The use of "psychology" in missions is at a crossroads, much like Philemon as he read Paul's letter to him. What was he to do with Onesimus? Roman law regarding slaves was clear. Paul was pleading for a new way—a new response. Resolve the conflict, with help from Apphia, Archippus, and the church. Welcome Onesimus to a new status. Acknowledge and embrace change and growth. As we face our future . . . what good advice!

## REFERENCE LIST

Beck, James R.
    1993    "Missions and Mental Health: A Lesson from History." *Journal of Psychology and Theology* 21(1): 9-17.

Carr, Karen L.
    1994    "Trauma and Post-Traumatic Stress Disorder among Missionaries: How to Recognize, Prevent, and Treat It." *Evangelical Missions Quarterly* 30: 246-255.

Dennett, Joan A.
    1990    "Let My People Grow." *Evangelical Missions Quarterly* 26: 146-152.

Hesselgrave, David J.
    1983    "Missionary Psychology and Counseling: A Timely Birth?" *Trinity Journal* 4: 72-81.
    1987    "Can Psychology Aid Us in the Fulfillment of the Great Commission? A Missiologist Speaks to Christian Psychologists." *Journal of Psychology and Theology* 15(4): 274-280.

Hunter, William F. and Marvin K. Mayers
    1987    "Psychology and Missions: Reflections on Status and Need." *Journal of Psychology and Theology* 15(4): 269-273.

O'Donnell, Kelly S.

1986 "Community Psychology and Unreached Peoples: Applications to Needs and Resource Assessment." *Journal of Psychology and Theology* 14(3): 213-223.

1987 "Developmental Tasks in the Life Cycle of Mission Families." *Journal of Psychology and Theology* 15(4): 281-290.

1988 "A Preliminary Study of Psychologists in Missions." In *Helping Missionaries Grow: Readings in Mental Health and Missions*. Edited by Kelly S. O'Donnell and Michelle O'Donnell. Pasadena, CA: William Carey Library.

Powell, John

1995 Personal Communication.

Ritchey, Janice K. and Christopher H. Rosik

1993 "Clarifying the Interplay of Developmental and Contextual Issues in Counseling Missionaries." *Journal of Psychology and Christianity* 12(2): 151-158.

Tucker, Ruth and L. Andrews

1992 "Historical Notes on Missionary Care." In *Missionary Care: Counting the Cost for World Evangelization*. Edited by Kelly S. O'Donnell. Pasadena, CA: William Carey Library.

# 6

# THE CONTRIBUTION OF TECHNOLOGY TO MISSIOLOGY

## Ron Rowland[1]

In examining the contribution of technology to missiology, this paper looks at recent trends in technology, their impact upon missiology, and the consequences of this upon missionary practice.

## TECHNOLOGY — RECENT TRENDS

In 1968, Warren R. Schilling wrote an article on "Technology and International Relations."[2] In it he identified four trends in technology:

1. "Science now precedes technology."
2. "Scientific knowledge and technological innovation are increasing at an exponential rate."
3. "Both the costs of acquiring new scientific knowledge and the costs of product innovation appear to be increasing."
4. "Scientific research has become increasingly subject to government control."

I will seek to comment on these from a 1995 perspective.

---

[1] Ron Rowland works at SIL
[2] Warren R. Schilling, "Technology and International Relations," in *Encyclopedia of Social Sciences* (Macmillan, 1968).

## Technology — Development and Science

Schilling's statement that "Science now precedes technology" is still partly true. He observed that whereas technology had always been the spur to drive scientific discovery, scientific discovery was now the driving force to dictate technological development. Science is making great advances, and does sometimes come first. However, the development of technology, with its consequent pressure on science, continues to grow. The growth is cyclical, with science and technology pushing each other forward. There appears to be an insatiable demand for the development of new technology. There is also an increased awareness of the impact of what has been called the "Wetware" factor. These factors, in their turn, drive scientific discovery.

*Technology—The Scope Of Development.*

The topic of technology is vast, and great strides have been made in many areas. Advances in travel and transportation have greatly changed our mission programs. Advances in health and medicine have increased effectiveness of ministry. Other areas of technology have contributed, but one area of technical advance stands out from all the others. That area is computing and electronic communication.

In his book *Technotrends*[3] Daniel Burrus lists twenty core technologies shaping the future. Of these, fourteen are directly related to the area of computing and electronic communication. These are listed below. The sub-sections indicate new products and services that will, I believe, profoundly alter the way we work. These products are already here or are in the pipeline and headed our way.

1. Digital Electronics
   a) Digital Imaging
   b) Digital Interactive Television
   c) Digital Cellular Telephones
   d) PersonalCommunication Networks

---

[3]Daniel Burrus, *Technotrends* (New York: Harper Business, 1993), 1-376.

2. Optical Data Storage
   a) Advanced compact disks
   b) Holographic crystals (future)
3. Advanced Video Displays
   a) Advanced flat-panel displays
   b) High definition television (future)
4. Advanced Computers
   a) Electronic notepads
   b) Multimedia computers
   c) Telecomputer
   d) Parallel processing computers
5. Distributed Computing
   a) Electronic data exchange
   b) Desktop videoconferencing
   c) Local area networks
   d) Wide area networks
6. Artificial Intelligence
   a) Advanced expert systems
   b) Advanced simulations
   c) Object-oriented programming
   d) Fuzzy logic
   e) Neural networks
   f) Voice recognition
7. Lasers
   a) Advanced compact disks
   b) Holography
8. Fiber Optics
9. Microwaves
10. Advanced Satellites
    a) Low earth orbit satellites
    b) Direct broadcast satellites
11. Photovoltaic Cells
12. Micromechanics
13. New Polymers
    a) Mixed-media polymers
    b) Conductive polymers
14. Superconductors

It is this area of computing and electronic communication that is examined in this paper.

*The Impact of the "Wetware" Factor.*

In order to fill out our understanding of the expansion of technology we need to refer to what is known as wetware. "Wetware" is the human interaction with the technology which presses forward the advances that are made. Charles Babbage first developed the idea of an "analytical engine" because he was asked by the British government to develop a way of predicting the rise and fall of the tides.

*Calculating power* was the first driving force for computer development. As the demand for complexity grew, we saw the development of *parallel computing* and *multi-tasking*.

As textual information began to be stored, first as data and then in hyper-text form, the need grew for *integrated applications* and *comprehensive information access*.

Next came *graphics, full visual capability*, and *audio capability*.

Now we have a strong drive towards *near-site information access, interactive video-conferencing*, and *3D modeling*.

Along with this increased complexity has come a strong demand for *transparent technology* and *user-friendly applications*.

These are the growth areas (and the "buzz words") in software development and in the development of peripherals and associated technology. We can expect still more advances in these areas.

Allow me to make two interesting observations about "wetware" and the mission community:

> 1. It seems that two streams of information gathering have been going on. On the one side, driven by the need for strategic and management data, with a strong support from North American missions, evangelicals have developed strong skills and experience with "databases." Other groups, with a strong Euro-

pean influence, have focused on "bibliographic" information. Recently, there has been a merging of these activities by organizations such as Global Mapping International, with their 20/21 Library project.[4]

2. The strong drive for missions to link information to global outreach has meant that the mission community has developed a surprisingly strong presence in the area of mapping and global information about people. Mission community influence on the development of Geographic Information Systems is not insignificant. Some of the mapping capabilities with regard to base maps, peoples and languages, people habitats, etc., are sufficiently accurate and comprehensive as to be of considerable interest in the secular geospatial community.

*Technology—The Rate of Increase.*

The second trend observed by Schilling contends that "Scientific knowledge and technical innovation are increasing at an exponential rate." We have seen the truth of this, and wonder how to diagram "exponential" now, as opposed to 1968! First, we need to consider the context, recalling the outstanding revolution that has taken place. The following diagram shows the increased pace and complexity as we move from the Industrial Age, through the Information Age, into what some are now calling the Communications Age.

| INDUSTRIAL AGE | INFORMATION AGE | COMMUNICATIONS AGE |
|---|---|---|
| 1750  /// 1950  1960 | 1970   1980 | 1990  1995 |
| - 21 decades - | - 2 decades - | ? - |

---

[4] Christopher Smith, "Mission Research and the Path to CD-ROM: Report on the Global Quest to Share Information," *International Bulletin of Missionary Research*, October 1995.

Secondly, we trace the rate of development of computer hardware and software, and electronic communications.

*Development of Hardware*

1832  Charles Babbage was asked by the British Government to devise a method for measuring the rise and fall of the tides. He designed his "Analytical Machine," but found that the technology was not yet adequate for full development of the model.
1941  First Relay Computer.
1944  The Electronic Numerical Integrator And Calculator. ENIAC—the first modern computer. It weighed over thirty tons, measured 3,000 square feet, consumed 140,000 watts of electricity, and could execute up to 5,000 basic arithmetic operations per second.
1975  350,000 computers. First personal computer developed.
1981  First IBM personal computer.
1983  Two million personal computers.
1992  486 microprocessor. It is built on a tiny piece of silicon about the size of a dime. It weighs less than a packet of Sweet'NLow, and uses less than two watts of electricity. A 486 can execute up to 54,000,000 instructions per second.[5]
1993  Sixty-five million personal computers.

*Development of Software*

1950s  First software monitor.
1970s  CPM, DOS, Apple.
1980s  Graphical User Interface; Vizualization; Multi-Tasking
1990s  Integrated Suites; Windows NT; OS/2; Desktop On-line Non-linear Video Editing; Win'95.

---

[5] Price Pritchett, *The Employee Handbook Of New Work Habits For A Radically Changing World* (Dallas: Pritchett & Associates, 1994).

*Development of Communications*

| | |
|---|---|
| 1876 | Invention of telephone. |
| 1958 | First satellite broadcast. |
| 1960 | Packet-switching networks. |
| 1969 | Internet began with four host sites. |
| 1984 | 1,000 host sites. |
| 1986 | 100,000 host sites. |
| 1992 | One million host sites. |
| 1992 | World Wide Web. |
| 1994 | Measurement of Internet participation changes to reflect new complexity:<br>Core Internet—WWW host sites: 7.8 million.<br>add: Consumer Internet—includes WWW users: 13.5 million.<br>add: the Matrix—includes e-mail users, et al.: 27.5 million. |

**Technology—The Cost**

The third trend described by Schilling observes that "[b]oth the costs of acquiring new scientific knowledge and the costs of product innovation appear to be increasing." In many ways this is still true. And yet significant changes are occurring. I am not an economist, but several observations are apparent to me.

a. With the end of the cold war, an increased emphasis upon cooperation, and the expansion of the "virtual community"; some costs, though by no means all, are mitigated by increased sharing across organizational and national boundaries, and a more open access to scientific knowledge and technology.

b. The opportunity for the sharing and acquisition of knowledge is much greater, and the timing of such sharing is much more immediate. The cost of sharing knowledge seems to be considerably less.

c. Costs for scientific research and product development are still high, yet many breakthroughs, as always, occur outside of the political-industrial establishment. There remains an interesting balance between the research and development establishment and the entrepreneurial individual or small shop.

d. Equipment costs in the computing sector have deceased dramatically, while processing power has increased to new heights. This makes it possible for scientific research and knowledge acquisition to be distributed and decentralized, with a decrease in operating costs.

**Technology—Who Controls It?**

Schilling's fourth observed trend was that "[s]cientific research has become increasingly subject to government control."

Again, there are several factors that have modified, and to some extent reversed, this trend.

a. A lowering of political barriers has made the sharing of research more possible.

b. Global sharing of information, and the speed at which it can be accomplished, undermine the possibility of exerting control.

c. There is an international trend to practice networking and develop strategic alliances between government, academic, business, and voluntary organizations.

With the introduction of the Internet in 1969, ARPANET was formed to share information. Universities and government were involved together from the beginning. In 1981, BITNET increased the capability and the variety of agency involvement. In 1992 the Internet Society was formed as a non-governmental co-operative organization.

Now, government is again trying to reach the pilot's seat—or at least to be co-pilot, or navigator!

In 1993, the US government saw private sector firms already developing a form of infrastructure in an ad-hoc manner.

> That is why the Administration has launched the National Information Infrastructure Initiative. We are committed to working with business, labor, academia, public interest groups, Con-

gress, and state and local government to ensure the development of a national information infrastructure (NII) which enables all Americans to access information and communicate with each other using voice, data, image or video at anytime anywhere.

At the same time, a National Spatial Data Infrastructure was being developed for geo-spatial information. This drew together several different existing networks and affiliations.

As other countries also developed NIIs, Vice President Al Gore, in March 1994, advanced the concept of a Global Information Infrastructure (GII) in a speech to the ITU World Tele-communication Development Conference in Buenos Aires, Argentina.

The Administration is considering options for pursuing further international dialogue and cooperation on the GIUI in both bilateral and multilateral venues.

**Recent Trends—Summary**

Twenty-seven years later we look at the four trends that Schilling identified.

1. Science and technology are still pushing each other forward to new areas of discovery.

2. Scientific knowledge and technological innovation, together cause exponential increase.

3. Cost is still a significant factor, but much of the impact of it is widely dispersed.

4. The struggle for control still goes on between governmental and non-governmental forces.

# TECHNOLOGY—
# ITS IMPACT UPON MISSIOLOGY

The impact of technology upon mission, and missiology, has been powerful and pervasive. The area of information systems has become increasingly complex, and I have developed a matrix model to try to manage the complexity. I have chosen to define this in terms of five areas of activity in missions information: information gathering, application, presentation, communication and administration. In each of these activity areas there needs to be consideration of data, technology, institutions and standards. The following observations follow this model in general, but without the differentiation of the matrix.

**Information Gathering**

The gathering of information has been greatly enhanced by the technology now available. More agencies and individuals have become information gatherers, on more topics, and in more places. There is a vast amount of information being compiled both inside and outside of the mission community.

The software needed for information gathering is adequate, and is now being enhanced with increasingly powerful laptop computers, and such additions as Global Positioning Systems.

Vigorous debates are taking place about definitions, validity, security, confidentiality, ownership, intellectual property rights, copyright and appropriateness of information. A code of conduct has been developed by SHARE Fellowship in its Information Sharing Handbook. This is being adopted by a growing number of agencies, but is still not well known, nor is it always observed.

**Information Application**

The application of information has been slower in developing. I believe that the principal road-block, however, is not technical. It lies in the reluctance, and/or lack of skill, of the mission executive to imaginatively utilize the software and technical help available.

In the area of business applications the software is available in abundance—word processors, spreadsheets, databases, hypertext systems, project managers, contact managers, accounting software, business management software, file management systems, geographic information systems, and others.

Many of these are now available not only as "stand-alones," but as "integrated packages," such as Claris Works, or Microsoft Works for Windows '95, or as fully developed "software suites" such as Microsoft Office Professional for

Windows, Lotus's SmartSuite 3.1 for Windows, or Novell Perfect Office for Windows.

There are software packages that assist in organizational management and decision-making, but these are not so popular or, in my judgment, so helpful for the mission executive.

**Information Presentation**

Again, the technology for information presentation is, in most cases, far ahead of the use to which mission agencies put it. Some of the obstacles are financial, but more often the lack of development can be attributed to the human element. There are progressive individuals, and even some progressive organizations, but in general usage is very ordinary and unimaginative.

There are now several relatively low-cost presentation packages, such as Astound, Microsoft Power-Point, Freelance Graphics, and WordPerfect Presentations. For those who are more ambitious, graphics programs include ABC Graphics Suite for Windows, Corel Draw, Harvard Graphics, and many others. Many of these packages can now be used in association with video and sound. Use of video is now still further advanced by desktop non-linear video editing.

Presentations can be interactive, and supported by CD-ROM technology. Some are considering the communication of presentations directly to churches, colleges, etc., by means of the Internet.

More expensive and technically demanding options also exist. Some in the missions community are looking at large-screen presentations combining recent advances in presentation technology with more powerful graphics software, geographic information systems, satellite imagery, and 3D "fly through" technology.

**Information Communication**

This is an area that has exploded in recent years. Several missions now have their own internationally operated e-mail systems.

Mission Aviation Fellowship and CrossConnect have now opened this possibility to many more in the mission community.

Brigada has opened wide the area of electronic conferencing for missions.

The number of Christian and mission home pages on Internet's World Wide Web is constantly increasing.

There are many remaining challenges, such as the secure and reliable transmission of large files, graphics files, etc., but, as demand increases, so do the technical solutions made available.

This is one of the most significant new areas of the contribution of technology to missiology. We will examine some of the implications and consequences of this movement in the section "Technology—The Consequences for Missiology" in this paper.

**Information Administration**

The topic of administration of information systems and technology is multi-faceted. Much of this is being handled within mission organizations, but a growing amount of information management must be addressed at the inter-organizational level. Such groups as SHARE Fellowship and Peoples Information Network have played a part in this within the mission community.

There have been several movements recently in the broader information community to apply some kind of order to an increasingly chaotic situation.

Several countries have sought to develop national information infrastructures,[6] and a serious attempt is now being made to integrate these into a global information infrastructure.[7]

Several mission organizations (as GMIN) are currently examining the possibility of a global mission information infrastructure.[8]

---

[6] http://www.cpsr.org/cspr/nii/nii_policy

[7] http://www.cspr.org/cspr/nii/ntia.doc.gov:70/0/papers/documents/gii_update.txt

[8] Ron Rowland, *What is GMIN?* (Dallas: Peoples Information Network, 1995).

# TECHNOLOGY—
# THE CONSEQUENCES FOR MISSIOLOGY

The impact of technology on missiology has been significant, and will become increasingly so. We need to see this from a Christian perspective, and recognize that "all human culture is now east of Eden and, so, subject to the aberrations and adulterations of human autonomy."[9] We need to recognize some of the consequences that have occurred, and that continue to occur, and examine our responsibilities. In the words of Francis Schaeffer:

> The Christian is to resist the spirit of the world. But when we say this we must understand that the world-spirit does not always take the same form. So the Christian must resist the spirit of the world in the form it takes in his own generation. If he does not do that he is not resisting the spirit of the world at all.[10]

I do not consider myself an expert in this area, but offer these observations as a concerned citizen. They are not exhaustive, but illustrate the challenges that we face.

### Consequences for Community

Electronic communication develops among users a sense of *virtual community*. This is one of its strengths. Communication can take place in new ways.

Distances of hundreds or thousands of miles no longer prevent almost instant communication. There can be, and soon will be for many more of us, interactive video teleconferencing. There are tremendous and clearly perceivable benefits. There is a sense in which electronic communication can supplant the barriers of time and space.

---

[9]Douglas Groothuis, *Technology's Subtle Assault on the Personal* (Focal Point), 3-6.

[10]Francis A. Schaeffer, *The God Who is There. Speaking Historic Christianity into the Twentieth Century* (Downers Grove, IL: InterVarsity Press, 1968).

There is, however, also a sense in which electronic communication can supplant face-to-face communication. People can "meet" in cyberspace who have no other association. It can simulate the personal dimension while actually subverting it. The effects are subtle, but profound. Not all are bad, but all need to be recognized.

- In the business environment, the representative of a Fortune 500 company competes on a level playing field with the operator of a home office operation. Only the product or service offered is seen and evaluated on screen.
- In the mission environment, the representative of a large agency, grounded in an illustrious history, and reflecting impressive past achievements, is measured only by the impact and appeal of his latest contribution. It must compete with any and all comers.
- Participants in an electronic conference often seek to become a "committee of the whole," and desire to participate in decisions that may not be theirs to make, and for which they hold no on-going responsibility. There can be an enormous sense of power in being on line.
- Those in conference become the "in community," and there is often a significant absence of non-technical players.
- The potential for international participation is theoretically strong, but in reality there is a marked lack of representation.
- There is a danger of domination and undue influence which must be countered by universal and affordable access. This subject of access is worth separate consideration (see "The Challenge of Access" below).
- It has been observed that "with this faceless exchange of data, net users are known to become rude and unmannerly." Sadly, this lack of Christian courtesy is sometimes true on Christian conferences and forums also.

There is a sense in which greater interaction also uncovers more of our "ethnocentric," and even "ideocentric," motivation. (Someone has even coined the term "ergo-centric" to describe those who are centered on "the task"!)

Such motivation is not inherently bad. God does give us differences of vision, ministry, and purpose. We do, however, need to learn the value of plurality of functions, and to be more willing to accept ambiguity and uncertainty.

Networking is a strong perceived value in the mission community. It is less of a real value in practice. It has been my observation that we are not very good at networking.

This problem of "practicing the Body" is not peculiar to the technical environment, but it is a very real challenge on the human side of technology.

I pray and hope that the development of a Global Mission Information Network (GMIN) is one of the pro-active movements that is taking place at this time (See Rowland, *What is GMIN?*). The mission community seeks to define ways in which the "virtual community," as a reflection of the mission community, can operate in a continuous learning mode to serve the mission community.

May God give us the grace to be the church in this worldwide context.

## Consequences For Information

Again, the potential is enormous, and the ability to obtain more direct, and more timely, information is attractive. I do not deny the benefits, and I am a constant proponent and encourager of database development, and better access to on-line information. However, we need to be informed users, aware of the subtle change that can occur to information shared on-line.

- Making information available on computer, or on-line, can sometimes blur the intent of the original author. It creates a "stockpile of malleable materials subject to the whim of the hypertext operator." It can more easily be taken out of context, and the original meaning can, deliberately or accidentally, be significantly altered.
- Subtleties of humor, or other expressions of emotion, are frequently misinterpreted, and sometimes the results are themselves humorous or tragic.
- The immediate and voluminous availability of information carries risks with regard to validity and integrity. Some information is not adequately researched; some is "edited" or "corrected"—often without change of attribution so that no one knows where the "editing" took place. There is an urgent need to develop measures to ensure accountability, validation, etc.

- The disregard for intellectual property rights, and appropriate acknowledgment of source, seemingly increases in this non-personal environment.
- Privacy and confidentiality are frequently compromised, but through conferencing, or on the Web, the audience is often much larger and less well-informed.

**The Challenge of Access.**

One of the consequences of the technology explosion is the danger of widening the gap between the haves and have-nots. This, of course, is not only a majority world problem. There is an ever-widening gap in advanced countries between those who have embraced technology, and those who have not, for whatever reason. It is, however, also a problem between nations, and between ministries based in different nations.

- There is a vast and growing *technological gap*. The Internet Society Map of International Connectivity[11] is very revealing. The continent of Africa stands out, in particular, as lacking good connectivity. The map, of course, only shows country connectivity status and does not begin to reflect the further difficulties within certain countries.
  There is, however, a way to at least reduce this gap. MAF/CrossConnect are developing satellite connections which can overcome lack of connectivity.[12] Will the mission community take up the challenge and take steps to bridge this gap?
- There is also a substantial *training gap*. This is partly a matter of technological training, often with the need for our older generation to first overcome technology aversion.
  This gap will be increased as the next generation of missionaries becomes involved. Many more of them, from the advantaged countries will be not just computer literate but computer functional. Computers are now introduced in primary school, and some students operate "virtual reality" labs in high school.
  However, the training gap also reflects different cultural approaches to decision-making and learning. The technology

---

[11] http://info.isoc.org:80/images/mapv14.gtf
[12] MAFnet 1995.

has been developed within the context of Western culture. Some aspects of this are being examined by the mission community, but far more needs to be done if culturally appropriate technologies are to be available.
- Then, there is the *economic gap*. Let me briefly mention two areas that need to be addressed.

First, there is the fundamental problem of distribution of wealth. This is not a new problem, but it is enhanced by the cost of equipment, software and services. So, the gap continues to widen, and the unity of the church is impeded.

Second, there is the on-going debate about financial charges for information. Should mission organizations seek to cover development or administrative costs from other mission organizations? Should there be differential charges according to the ability of the customer to pay? What about Internet costs? Information on the Internet is traditionally free. There is, however, a growing debate about the appropriateness of this. Where should missions stand on this?

## CONCLUSION

I have sought to show that technology is changing the face of missions and will continue to do so at an ever-increasing rate. I believe that we need to see this change as a positive factor, and one which God can use to further empower the mission community to accomplish his purposes.

At the same time, we live in a fallen world. We ignore at our peril the consequences that accompany such change. You will observe that the paper raises many questions, but offers few answers. I do not have the answers. I believe, however, that the contribution of technology to missiology should remind us again that our dependence is on God.

May our prayer be that of Solomon:

> I am only a little child and do not know how to carry out my duties. Your servant is here among the people you have chosen, a great people, too numerous to count or number. So give your servant a discerning heart to govern your people and to distinguish between right and wrong. For

who is able to govern this great people of yours? (1Ki 3:7-9)

# 7

# ECONOMICS AND MISSION

## Andreas J. Köstenberger[1]

### ECONOMICS AND MISSION: A CRITICAL RELATIONSHIP

Economics and mission interface at many crucial junctures. While mission is still frequently treated in isolation from socio-economic factors, the failure to adequately deal with such realities and their impact on mission renders those involved in the missionary enterprise ill-equipped to cope with the increasingly complex circumstances affecting the propagation of the Christian gospel world-wide. Put simply, economics pertains to the allocation of limited resources. It is apparent that economic decisions need to be made both on a macro- and on a micro-level in the process of missionary strategy and deployment. For the purposes of this essay, we may define Christian mission as the church's modelling and proclamation of the gospel message. In the following essay, we will first look at mission-economic highlights in biblical history before discussing the contemporary economic implications for mission. This will be followed by four specialized sections, dealing with the relationship between the "Great Commandment" and the "Great Commission" and the issues of debt, consumerism, and sociological barriers, all of which present serious potential obstacles to Christian mission.

---

[1] Andreas J. Köstenberger teaches New Testament.

## Scripture and Economics

From the earliest days of God's dealings with his people, it is clear that God's call ought to take priority over an individual's loyalties to those around him. Abraham, the father of believers, was called to leave his home, even to sacrifice his son; the other patriarchs, likewise, were enjoined to live by faith (He 11:8-22). Moses, too, chose to renounce his earthly possessions (He 11:24-28), and the abandonment of self-pursuits was required of the Old Testament prophets. The same principle is reflected in the New Testament in Christ's own self-emptying (Php 2:7), his selfless service (Mk 10:45; Jn 13:1-15), and his becoming poor to make believers rich (2Co 8:9). Such sacrifice also became the requirement for discipleship (Lk 9:57-62; Jesus' stewardship parables).

Of the four evangelists, it is Luke who shows the greatest interest in economic issues (Lk 4:18-21 quoting Isa 61:1-2; cf. Lk 6:20 with Mt 5:3). Luke's account of the life of the early church in Acts provides an eschatological foretaste of kingdom living (Ac 2:44-45; 4:32-37). Paul, likewise, emulated self-sacrifice in his own life and ministry, calling believers to the sharing of resources with those in need (esp. the collection for the Jerusalem church: Ro 15:25-27; 1Co 16:1-4; 2Co 8-9), contentment with life's necessities (Php 4:11-12; 1Ti 6:6-8; cf. Mt 6:11; Lk 11:3), a disinterested attitude toward worldly possessions (1Co 7:30-31), and hospitality (Ro 12:13). Christianity is to transform slavery from the inside out (Phm; 1Co 7:21-24).

Believers were to extend hospitality to missionaries and itinerant preachers of the gospel (Mt 10:10-15; He 13:2; 2Jn 10-11; 3Jn 5-8). Fundamental to missions is the acknowledgment that Christians are merely resident aliens and that this world is not their permanent abode (Php 3:20; 1Pe 1:1,17; 2:11). The love of money is the root of all evil (1Ti 6:10; cf. Mk 4:18-19; 1Ti 3:3; 2Ti 3:2), no one can serve two masters, God and money (Mt 6:24), and rich persons will enter the kingdom only with great difficulty (Mk 10:23-31; Lk 12:16-21; 16:19-31; 19:1-10; 1Ti 6:17-19; Jas 5:1-6; Davids). In the seer's apocalyptic vision, Babylon the Great, with its excessive reliance on her own wealth, has fallen (Re 17-18).

**Economics and Mission: An Overview**

The Christian missionary enterprise is faced with issues pertaining to economics at many points. The following questions are particularly significant: (1) the general economic environment for mission (Bonk) and the question of which economic system is most compatible with biblical principles (Chewning, Novak, Smith); (2) the economic situation of missionaries, including the raising of funds, "tentmaking," the problem of fluctuating currency exchange rates, the problem of financial indebtedness of missionary candidates, and the issue of greater cost-efficiency of national missionaries (Yohannan); (3) the economic circumstances of the target cultures of mission, raising issues such as the need for community development and relief work, sociological barriers between the missionary and nationals, the need for economic support of new converts ostracized from their socio-economic community, and the problem of indigenous churches' dependence on foreign funds.

Of contemporary movements, it is particularly liberation theology that focuses on economic issues, usually in terms of Marxist economic analysis (Novak 287-97). The following factors, however, appear to contradict this approach (France): first, Jesus conceived of his own role not in terms of political or national liberation but of the restoration of an individual's personal relationship with God; he explicitly re-jected a political role, stressing rather love and forgiveness even of one's enemies, an element frequently missing in radi-cal movements; second, liberation in the New Testament al-most always pertains to liberation from sin; third, Jesus does not present a programme for achieving the redistribution of wealth or other socio-economic reforms; and fourth, liberation theology concentrates on the symptom of socio-economic justice while neglecting to deal with the root cause, i.e. the fallenness of human nature, which produces the twisted values of selfish materialism.

A sensitivity to economic issues is vital for the church's effective ministry. The world's rapid urbanization, the evolution of modern technologies creating a new information elite, the increasing gap between rich and poor countries, and many other factors affect the church's ministry at home and abroad in many ways. Evangelical spokesmen such as R. Sider and A. Campolo have called for a more simple, radical life-style on the part of Christians for the sake of missions. It has been the subject of considerable debate in evangelical circles over the last decades to what extent social and economic concerns are to be part of the missionary enterprise. Some advocate the priority of evangelism and church-planting, while others favor a holistic approach that also incorporates social and economic issues (see further "Great Commandment and Great Commission" below). Many favor an approach that is patterned after the model of Christ's incarnation and service (Stott; but see Köstenberger).

Another crucial issue is a proper allocation of resources that allows unreached or little reached people groups to hear the gospel. Currently, Christians are allocating only 1.2% of their mission funding to the 1.3 billion people who live in the least-evangelized world. Over 90% of foreign missionaries, 87% of mission funding, and over 94% of full-time Christian workers are directed toward those countries where at least 60% of the population identify themselves as Christians (Siewert and Kenyon). This hardly seems to be a wise allocation of resources. A major revision of spending priorities is in order.

Moreover, the cost of sending Western missionaries is considered by some to be "scandalous" and "increasingly prohibitive" (Siewert and Kenyon, 35). The typical model of the American missionary agency presupposes and requires large financial resources for the deployment of missionaries as well as for the agencies' administration (Siewert and Kenyon, 52). Moreover, the adaptation of free market approaches to missionary practices is increasingly viewed as problematic. The establishment of a strategy, aiming at growth and success, including specific goals along a clearly delineated time-table, may be more a product of American pragmatism than reflect biblical values and principles. A critical re-evaluation of this approach is long overdue.

The following implications for modern missions emerge from these considerations: (1) biblical discipleship, the prerequisite for missions, entails a disinterested attitude toward worldly possessions (1Co 7:30-31); (2) material resources are to be used for the spreading of God's kingdom (Jesus' kingdom and stewardship parables); (3) solidarity is called for between believers of different means in local churches and across cultures, leading to a sharing of resources (2Co 8-9); (4) the ultimate issues in missions are spiritual, but economic and social factors may provide barriers to effective evangelization (Bonk; see also "Sociological Barriers" below); (5) the proper allocation of financial and other resources to mission is an important aspect of the church's Christian stewardship and should be carefully monitored to reflect biblical priorities; it should be acknowledged that missionary "delivery systems" are culturally constrained and thus should be modified in different cultures and times rather than perpetrated in form when their function has changed (viz. readings of the book of Acts); (6) all missions work takes place in a political, economic, and social environment, and these factors influence the accomplishment of the missionary task (Clouse). After this survey, we now turn to several specific issues involving economics and mission.

## ISSUES INVOLVING ECONOMICS AND MISSION

### The Great Commission and the Great Commandment

When considering missions, it is usually not the Great Commandment (Mk 12:28-34 par. Mt 22:34-40; cf. Lk 10:25-28) but the Great Commission (Mt 28:16-20; Lk 24:46-49) that takes center stage. Arguably, however, the Great Commandment provides a crucial foundation for the Great Commission, and a unilateral emphasis on the latter creates an imbalance that may render the church's mission ineffective. We will first discuss the scriptural foundation for the Great Commandment and subsequently deal with its contemporary relevance for mission.

*Scriptural Foundation*

The Great Commandment, according to Jesus, is the Old Testament command to love God with all of one's heart, soul, mind, and strength (Dt 6:4-5), together with the injunction to love one's neighbor as oneself (cf. Lev 19:18b; on the question of who is one's "neighbor," cf. Lev 19:34; Lk 10:25-27; and Mt 5:43-48). To call this commandment the Great Commandment is to follow Matthew's terminology (Mt 22:36: "great"; 22:38: "great and first"), where "great" is probably used with elative force to denote what is "greatest" or "most important." Mark simply numbers the commandments as "first" and "second" (Mk 12:38,41; cf. Mt 22:38). In Luke, the lawyer's question is, "Teacher, what shall I do to inherit eternal life?" (Lk 10:25), raising the question of whether Luke's account refers to a different event altogether, especially since, in Luke, it is not Jesus who is speaking but the lawyer (Lk 10:27).

The question of what constituted the heart of the Law was an issue widely discussed in rabbinic circles in Jesus' day. Jesus' emphatic statement, only found in Matthew, that the entire Law and the Prophets depend on the Great Commandment is therefore of utmost significance (Mt 22:40). Unlike the Decalogue, which is mostly given in the form of prohibitions, Jesus states this injunction in a positive way (cf. Mt 7:12). By expressing the commandment in an absolute and categorical rather than a relative and limited fashion, Jesus stresses the priority of the inward disposition over the outward action. In keeping with Old Testament prophetic tradition, Jesus requires heart religion, not merely formalistic legalism. At the same time, it is not his desire to use this commandment to relegate every other obligation of the believer to the point of irrelevance.

What is the relationship between the Great Commandment and the Great Commission in Matthew's gospel? Since Matthew presents discipleship as the "way of righteousness" (cf. Mt 5:6,10,20; 6:33), and since the Great Commission entails the teaching of converts to obey everything Jesus commanded, it is clear that the keeping of the Great Commandment is a prerequisite for the fulfillment of the Great Commission. Moreover, the latter entails, not mere "evangelism" in modern parlance, where the term usually refers merely to the bringing of a person to the point of conversion, but the grounding of Christian converts in "the way of righteousness," including the observance of the Great Commandment (and, ultimately, once again the Great Commission!). Finally, the concept of righteousness in Matthew, while possessing a spiritual core, is not limited to the religious domain but also has social and economic dimensions. In these ways Matthew lays a crucial foundation for the understanding of the relationship between the Great Commandment and the Great Commission in contemporary discussion.

## Contemporary Relevance for Mission

Historically, Anglo-Saxon Protestant missionary thought has emphasized the Great Commission, while the task never occupied an equally central position among Christians on the European continent. In recent years, the issue of the relationship between the Great Commission and the Great Commandment caused considerable discussion at the Lausanne Congress in 1974. While in the final conference document evangelism was named as the primary mission of the church, this drew the criticism of a significant number of participants, including J. Stott, R. Sider, and others. After a reaffirmation of the primacy of evangelism by the Consultation on World Evangelization (COWE) in Pattaya, Thailand, in June 1980, the question was taken up again by the Consultation on the Relationship between Evangelism and Social Responsibility held in Grand Rapids, Michigan, in June of 1982, an effort co-sponsored by the World Evangelical Fellowship (WEF) and the Lausanne Committee for World Evangelization (LCWE). This conference identified three kinds of relationships between evangelism and the church's social responsibility: (1) social responsibility as a consequence of evangelism; (2) social action as a bridge to evangelism; and (3) social concern as a partner of evangelism. The delegates advocated a holistic approach to mission, since "[s]eldom if ever should we have to choose between satisfying physical hunger and spiritual hunger, or between healing bodies or saving souls, since an authentic love for our neighbor will lead us to serve him or her as a whole person."

The key questions addressed at the 1982 consultation were: What is mission? How broad is salvation in Scripture? What is the relationship between the church and the kingdom? and What is the church's mandate for social justice? R. Sider and J. I. Packer, in contrast to the World Council of Churches (WCC) at its 1973 meeting in Bangkok, argued for a narrow use of salvation language, restricting salvation "to the sphere of conscious confession of faith in Christ." A. Johnston, D. McGavran, P. Wagner, P. Beyerhaus, K. Bockmuehl, and H. Lindsell joined in affirming this position against those who sought to define salvation more broadly. This latter group contended that salvation has not only personal but also social and cosmic dimensions, so that socioeconomic improvements should be described as an aspect of salvation, pointing also to Luke 4:16-21 (cf. Isa 61:1-2). It was further argued that the Lordship of Christ extends over all demonic powers of evil that "possess persons, pervade structures, societies, and the created order."

How does Scripture adjudicate between these two positions? On the one hand, it cautions against a reductionistic focus on people merely as "souls" that need to be saved, so that the church's task should not be narrowly conceived in merely "religious" terms. On the other hand, Scripture does affirm the primacy of a person's spiritual dimension, so that the effort of leading unbelievers to a Christian conversion rightly belongs at the heart of the church's mission. As noted, read in the context of Matthew's entire gospel, the fulfillment of the Great Commission entails a "commitment to both the King and his kingdom, to both righteousness and justice" (Bosch), while the making of disciples also involves teaching them to obey Jesus' teachings which include loving God and one's neighbor. Hence love for God and others ought to be the driving motivation for mission, since, in love, God sent his Son; in love, Jesus gave his life for others; and by our love, the world will know that we are his disciples.

## Consumerism

While it is not always recognized, consumerism presents a serious obstacle to Christian mission. The term may be used in reference to the movement sparked by Ralph Nader in the 1970s aimed at better information and protection of consumers, or as a rough synonym for American-style capitalism and materialism. Modern marketing, with its elevation of the consumer to pre-eminence, and with its development of sophisticated advertising techniques, has had a powerful impact on people's purchasing patterns in the West. Niche marketing and the segmentation of markets into smaller units has enabled companies to achieve greater distribution of their products, sometimes to the point of convincing people to buy goods they don't need but were merely made to want.

Consumerism is also an American export to many other parts of the world, such as the countries of Eastern Europe where people have been encouraged by various advertising and other marketing activities to express their cultural identity through spending, fostering a transition to cultures of consumption. If this trend continues, the American system of a consumer economy may become the model for the world economy, since traditional beliefs and customs of various cultural groups may not be strong enough to resist the spread of American popular culture. Indeed, the characteristics of American mass culture appear to make it an ideal culture for global cultural integration. Ultimately, however, both marketing and consumerism function within a capitalist, materialistic system, which is largely humanistic and devoid of ethical or spiritual values.

Vinay Samuel warns, "The market cannot be allowed such autonomy and dominance in shaping contemporary cultural values. The gospel of the kingdom must challenge and shape the forces of the market" (Siewert and Kenyon, 44). Indeed, it is alarming to what degree people in consumption-driven economies tie their identity and status to their spending. American popular culture, including television, clothing fashions, movies, fast food, sports, and music, is thoroughly materialistic and centers on consumerism. What is also problematic is that the American economy is tied to the current level of consumption to the extent that any significant decreases in personal spending would lead to an immediate recession.

Counter to this materialistic mind-set, Jesus taught that one's life does not consist of the multitude of one's possessions, cautioning people against greed that causes them to accumulate material possessions they cannot take with them when they die (Lk 12:15-21). Their treasure should be where their heart is (Mt 6:21 par. Lk 12:34). Those who wanted to follow Jesus were first encouraged to remember the poor and to give generously to meet their needs (Mt 19:21; Lk 19:8). Indeed, Jesus expected his followers to be prepared to renounce all of their possessions (Lk 14:33). A Christian is to consider his belongings to be resources entrusted to him by God to further his kingdom (Mt 24:45-51; 25:14-30; Lk 12:41-48; 16:1-13,19-25). Paul, likewise, preached modesty and contentment (Php 4:10-13; 1Ti 6:7-8).

Overall, the spirit of consumerism has led to greater personal debt and thus decreased missionary giving and deployment in recent years. As people are enculturated from childhood to expect a high level of physical comfort, they are more likely to give priority to meeting their own life-style needs than to sacrifice a substantial portion of their income for the cause of world evangelization. Missionaries themselves, likewise, may be affected in their life-style expectations. This has led some mission agencies to impose ceilings on outgoing expenses. In response to changing patterns of giving, some groups have begun to accentuate project over long-term giving, emphasizing also the benefits accrued to the one who chooses to invest in the support of missionaries. The high cost of Western-style missions also raises the issue of efficiency, which has led some to suggest the support of nationals instead of Western missionaries, surely a false dichotomy (Yohannan). Also, support requirements may be lessened through tentmaking or the willingness of missionaries to decrease their living standard expectations on the field (Bonk). In the final analysis, however, the solution is not to be found in the adaptation of surface strategies but in the preaching and the return to the attitudes toward material possessions urged by Jesus and Paul. Moreover, a rhythm of life that includes worship, prayer, rest, and time for relationships alongside work needs to be recovered in order to counteract the pervasive influence of materialistic values and to foster greater balance and harmony in people's lives.

**Debt**

Personal debt, incurred through the rising cost of education, consumer spending, or other means, likewise has become a serious obstacle to missionary recruitment and deployment in North America. While Scripture, contrary to the claims of some, does not forbid entering into debt altogether, it does warn against the bondage that may result from debt (Pr 22:7). Indeed, excessive debt presents a major barrier impeding people's ability to serve God and to do his work, including mission.

Christians have already been forgiven the ultimate debt they owe, i.e. sin before God (cf. esp. Mt 6:12 par. Lk 11:4; cf. also Lk 7:41-43; 16:1-13). God's gracious act of forgiveness of an astronomical debt (Mt 18:24: 10,000 talents=$10 million) should move us to forgive the debts (sins) of others (Mt 18:28: 100 denarii=0.00001% of 10,000 talents). Still, believers are called to wise stewardship of their financial and other resources. Their faithfulness or negligence will result in heavenly reward or loss. Moreover, in New Testament teaching, Christians' "debts" also include the fulfilling of one's obligations in marriage (1Co

7:3; Eph 5:28), as a citizen (Ro 13:7), in the preaching of the gospel (Ro 1:14), and in love and service of one's fellow-believers (Jn 13:14; Ro 13:8; 1Jn 3:16; 4:11).

The rising level of debt on the part of missionary candidates mirrors a general trend in the US economy that is characterized by escalating federal budget deficits, record credit card debts (1995: $3,900 per household; a 47% rise in 1994-95), and consumer spending increases without corresponding raises in salaries. Consumer spending fuels the entire American economic system, accounting for two-thirds of the economy, and life-style expectations continue to rise. Already Americans consume 40% of the world's natural resources while containing merely 5% of its population. If the Christian missionary movement in North America is unable to resist following this general economic trend, its demise as a major force in global missions may be imminent. In order to alleviate the burden of debt, some mission agencies currently allow a portion of missionaries' support to be devoted to the remission of debt (Coggins). Other groups encourage donors first to help candidates pay off their debts before supporting their missionary work. Many para-church and mission agencies allow staff members to remain on support while upgrading their education in exchange for a commitment to continued service with that organization.

Debt may be the result of a lack of contentment, one's inability to delay gratification, or other factors. While debt is not sin, it may result in bondage if it keeps a person from pursuing his or her calling from God. The church should act redemptively as well as pre-emptively: redemptively where significant debt has been incurred, pre-emptively in order to keep financial obligations resulting from educational and other expenses to a reasonable level.

## Sociological Barriers

Finally, we focus on the potential obstacle to Christian mission in the form of socio-economic barriers. In his day, Jesus admirably succeeded in breaking through social and economic barriers in order to reach people with the gospel. Huge crowds followed him. He accepted invitations by people from every stratum of society, ministered to the sick, the demon-possessed, Gentiles, women, children, and other groups awarded little or no status in his day. Yet Jesus' approach was not merely a method; it reflected a genuine attitude of the heart that all creatures are equally precious in the sight of God. Paul, likewise, was concerned to remove legitimate obstacles in order to maximize people's opportunity to hear the gospel. While being careful never to compromise the offense of the cross itself, Paul sought to "become all things to all men" in order to at least "save some" (1Co 9:19-23).

To this day, economic and sociological factors loom large in missionary proclamation. The church growth movement has advocated the "homogeneous unit" principle as well as a focus on receptive, responsive people groups to enhance the influx of new believers into the church. Brewster has urged missionaries to bond with nationals rather than being submerged in a missionary sub-culture. Bonk has recently examined disparities in living standards between Western missionaries and nationals. Greenway and others have advocated a simpler life-style for missionaries. Proponents of the church growth movement have alerted the missions world to the need of paying attention to sociological factors within the societies in which missionaries work. Mission work will be more effective if attention is paid to social stratification, homogeneous units, and webs of relationships. Homogeneous units are section[s] of society in which all the members have some characteristic in common (McGavran). These may include language or dialect, ways of life, standards, level of education, self-image, places of residence, and other characteristics. This insight has led later missiologists to define people groups as significantly large sociological grouping[s] of individuals who perceive themselves to have a common affinity for one another (Lausanne Committee for World Evangelization).

McGavran observed that people like to become Christians without crossing racial, linguistic, or class barriers. He concluded that church planters who enable people to become Christians without crossing such barriers are much more effective than those who place them in people's way, claiming support from the New Testament as well as church history. Not merely rational, denominational, and theological factors, but also environmental factors play a significant role in conversion. McGavran also noted that Americans are accustomed to a unified society and consequently do not like to face the fact that most human societies are stratified along socio-economic and other class lines. It should be noted, however, that some contend that church growth advocates assess people's receptivity too optimistically and that its methods are largely products of Western pragmatism and utilitarianism. On the North American scene, the rise of the "Willow Creek" phenomenon in the last twenty years has shown how the conscious removal of potential obstacles to church growth and the targeting of the gospel to specifical segments of culture may lead to significant, even explosive, church growth. At the same time, some have objected that even necessary obstacles to conversion and Christian growth have been removed. Indeed, care must be taken not to sanction capitalistic, self-serving life-styles and aspirations with the blessing of the gospel. Jesus' message to a similar audience would no doubt have been more confrontational and more radical than merely catering to people's needs while de-emphasizing the offensive elements of the Christian message.

Today missions has frequently become, not merely a calling from God, but a career. Missionaries have at times placed an undue emphasis on the securing of incomes, health insurance, and retirement benefits comparable to professionals in their home country. Moreover, it has become increasingly common for missionaries not to serve for a life-time but merely for a term, so that provision is made for circumstances conducive to their return home even before departure. Together with their dependence on foreign support while on the field, and the frequent requirement for them not to engage in formal employment while serving with a missions agency, barriers are erected which set many missionaries up for failure from the very outset. This is not to minimize legal requirements for residency in the respective countries where missionaries serve, nor to belittle the needs of missionaries. It does, however, call for a conscious return to the attitudes modeled by Jesus, Paul, and the early church, and for a conscious effort to remove legitimate economic and social barriers for the sake of those who are to be reached with the gospel.

## CONCLUSION

Together with the other social sciences, economics provides a crucial framework for the contemporary missionary enterprise. A complex web of factors pertain to mission, including the general economic environment for mission, the economic situation of missionaries, and the economic circumstances of the target cultures of mission. While economics should not be elevated to ultimate supremacy in one's theological system (viz. liberation theology), a failure to reckon with and to address economic issues will surely limit missionary effectiveness. In this essay, we focused particularly on the relationship between the Great Commission and the Great Commandment, a relationship that is to be held in fragile balance, as well as on a number of significant potential obstacles to mission, particularly consumerism, debt, and sociological barriers. Only some of the economic issues relating to mission could be surveyed. But it is hoped that even this brief survey will provide the impetus for further more detailed reflection on these and other questions vitally facing the church as it embarks on its mission at the verge of the twenty-first century.

## REFERENCE LIST

Bonk, J. J.
    1991    *Missions and Money: Affluence as a Western Missionary Problem.* Maryknoll, NY: Orbis.

Bosch, D. J.
    1984    "The Scope of Mission." *The International Review of Mission* 73: 17-32.

Carson, D. A.
    1984    "Matthew." In *Expositor's Bible Commentary*, ed. Frank E. Gaebelein Grand Rapids: Zondervan. Pp. 463-66.

Chewning, R. C., ed.
    1989    *Biblical Principles & Economics: The Foundations.* Colorado Springs: NavPress.

Clouse, R. G., ed.

    1984    *Wealth and Poverty: Four Christian Views.* Downers Grove: InterVarsity Press.

Coggins, W.

    1989    "Candidate debts: how significant a problem?" *Evangelical Missions Quarterly* 25: 262-68.

Davids, P. H.

    1992    "Rich and Poor." In *Dictionary of Jesus and the Gospels*, ed. J. B. Green, S. McKnight, and I. H. Marshall. Downers Grove: InterVarsity Press. Pp. 701-10.

Deiros, P. A.

    1985    "Evangelism and the Third World: The Great Commission and the Great Commandment." *Faith and Mission* 2: 42-49.

Engel, J.

    1996    *Finances of Missions.* Wheaton, IL: Stewardship Associates.

France, R. T.

    1986    "Liberation in the New Testament." *Evangelical Quarterly* 58: 3-23.

Fuller, R. H.

    1978    "The Double Commandment of Love: A Test Case for Authenticity." In *Essays on the Love Commandment*, ed. Luise Schottroff et al. Philadelphia: Fortress.

Greenway, R. S.

    1992    "Eighteen Barrels and Two Big Crates." *Evangelical Missions Quarterly* 28: 126-32.

Hartley, J. E.

    n.d.    "Debt." *ISBE* 1: 905-6.

Köstenberger, A. J.

    1995    "The Challenge of a Systematized Biblical Theology: Missiological Insights from the Gospel of John." *Missiology* 23: 445-64.

McGavran, D.

    1980    *Understanding Church Growth*. Grand Rapids: Eerdmans, 1970; rev. ed.

Novak, M.

    1991    *The Spirit of Democratic Capitalism*. Lanham, MD: Madison, [1982].

Peters, G. W.

    1981    *A Theology of Church Growth*. Grand Rapids: Zondervan.

Siewert, J. A. and J. A. Kenyon

    1995    *Mission Handbook*, 15th ed. Monrovia, CA: MARC.

Smith, I.

    1993    "God and Economics." In *God and Culture*, ed. D. A. Carson and John D. Woodbridge. Grand Rapids: Eerdmans. Pp. 162-79.

Stott, J. R. W.

    1975    *Christian Mission in the Modern World*. Downers Grove, IL: InterVarsity Press.

Wagner, C. P.

    1981    *Church Growth and the Whole Gospel*. San Francisco: Harper & Row.

Williamson, A. P.

    1982    "The Great Commission or the Great Commandment." *Christianity Today* 26 (19): 32-36.

Yohannan, K. P.

    1991    *Why the World Waits: Exposing the Reality of Modern Missions*. Lake Mary, FL: Creation House.

# PART II

# USE AND MISUSE OF THE SOCIAL SCIENCES

# 8

# A CRITIQUE OF CHARLES KRAFT'S USE/MISUSE OF COMMUNICATION AND SOCIAL SCIENCES IN BIBLICAL INTERPRETATION AND MISSIOLOGICAL FORMULATION

## Enoch Wan[1]

## INTRODUCTION

**Purpose**

This paper is written with a single purpose of providing a critique by answering the question whether Dr. Charles Kraft has used/misused the communication and social sciences in his biblical interpretation and missiological formulation.

**Methodology**

The generous cooperation of Dr. Kraft of Fuller Theological Seminary, in the provision of an updated comprehensive listing (see Appendix I for a sample of selected titles) of his published works, is gratefully acknowledged. His commitment and contribution to academic scholarship, missiological formulation, inter-disciplinary integration, etc. are much appreciated by many. In the last thirty some years, Dr. Kraft has written more than two dozen books (in areas ranging from linguistics, communication, missiology, to deliverance ministries, etc. with translations in Chinese, Korean, and German), and more than 120 articles, editorials and chapters in books.

---

[1]Enoch Wan is Professor of Missions and Anthropology at Reformed Theological Seminary.

From the list of Dr. Kraft's publications, it is obvious that there are three major foci traceable chronologically to his personal interest and professional development. From 1963-1973, he published seven volumes on Hausa, a Nigerian language. Beginning in article format in the early 1970s, his focus of research moved from linguistics/Bible translation to interdisciplinary integration of linguistics, hermeneutics, behavioral/social and communication sciences, etc., resulting in the publication of the influential and controversial book *Christianity in Culture* (1979a). (In the same year, two other books were published, *Readings in Dynamic Indigeneity* and *Communicating the Gospel God's Way*.) Since his exposure from 1982-1983 to demonology and deliverance ministries, by way of John Wimber's "Signs and Wonders" class at Fuller (Kraft 1987:122, 1989:6, 62) and his sub-sequent (or second, cf. Kraft 1979a:6-12 being his first) "paradigm shift" in 1984, his publications began to shift ("practice shift," 1987:127) towards that aspect of Christian ministries as marked by the publication of several titles of this nature: *Christianity with Power* (1989), *Defeating Dark Angels* (1992), *Deep Wounds, Deep Healing* and *Behind Enemy Lines* (both in 1994).

Of all the publications by Dr. Kraft, three books—i.e. *Christianity in Culture* (1979a), *Communication Theory for Christian Witness* (1983) and *Christianity with Power* (1989)—and several articles (see Appendix I) will be included as the most relevant and representative of his use/misuse of the communi-cation and social sciences in his biblical interpretation and mis-siological formulation.

## Definitions of Key Terms

*Bible:* The inspired truth of the sixty-six canonical books.

*Biblical Hermeneutics:* The principles and procedures by which the interpreter determines the meaning of the Holy Scripture within the proper contexts.

*Culture:* The context/consequence of patterned interaction of personal Beings/beings, in contrast to popular usage of culture applying to the presumed closed system of homo sapiens. This de-finition of culture can freely be applied or referred to angelic (fallen or good) beings of the angel-culture and the dynamic in-teraction of the Three Persons of the Triune God in theo-culture (Wan 1982b).

*Ethnohermeneutics:* The principles and procedures by which the interpreter determines the meaning of the Holy Scripture, inspired by the Primary Author (Triune God within theo-culture) and inscripturated through the secondary authors (human agents of varied historico-culturo-linguistic contexts of homino-culture) for the recipients (of varied historico-culturo-linguistic contexts) (Wan 1994).

*Inspiration:* The divine way of revealing biblical truth (the Bible) to humankind.

*Interpretation:* The human way of reducing distance and removing difference to ascertain the meaning of the text at hand (Berkhof 1969:11).

*Linguistic and Communication Sciences:* Includes the study of descriptive linguistics, applied linguistics, proxemic and kinesic communication, etc.

*Missiological Formulation:* The formation and de-velop-ment of theory/methodology/strategy for the sake of mission (the divine Great Commission) and missions (the human ways and means to fulfill the mission).

*Social sciences:* Includes disciplines such as sociology, anthropology, psychology, etc. and the term is used interchangeably with "behavioral sciences" in this study.

*Scriptural:* That which is taught by the Bible and is prescriptive, principle and transcultural/eternal in nature as compared to biblical—that which is found in the Bible and is of descriptive, precedent and cultural/temporal in nature (Wan 1994).

## KRAFT'S USE OF COMMUNICATION AND SOCIAL SCIENCES AS A CONTRIBUTION TO INTER-DISCIPLINARY INTEGRATION

With the advancement of modern scholarship comes the necessity of division of labor for the sake of specialization and the reality of the compartmentalization of knowledge and disciplines. In addition to the challenge of interdisciplinary integra-tion, Christian scholars have to take up the challenge of integra-ting their Christian faith with their efforts of interdisciplinary integration without injuring the integrity of either Christian faith (dogmatics; cf. warnings by David Hubbard, Kraft 1977:170; and Robert McQuilkin, 1977), academic disciplines (academics) or practical application (pragmatics).

For decades, evangelical Christians, like Charles Kraft in *Christianity in Culture: A Study in Dynamic Biblical Theolo-gizing in Cross-Cultural Perspective* (1979a), have successfully strived for multi-disciplinary integration, covering a multitude of subject matters. Of those, like Kraft, who have received similar professional training and with similar ministry experiences, have tried to bridge similar disciplines and covering similar top-ics, there are many, e.g. Eugene Nida, Kenneth Pike, Alan Tip-pett, William Wonderly, Linwood Barney, James O. Buswell, III, David Hesselgrave, Paul Hiebert, etc.

However, Kraft's book (1979a) is unique in terms of the combination of the following characteristics: conceptually coherent/consistent with simplicity (some reviewers like Carl Henry and Edward Gross may disagree on this point; yet it can be demonstrated as shown in Figures 1 and 2 below), "well-documented and carefully organized" (Henry 1980:153), thought provoking (Adeney 1980:24), "creative . . . challenging. Impressive . . . admirable" (Saayman 1981:89-90), innovative in theoretical formulation, illustrative in field experience, practical in illustrations, comprehensive in coverage, etc.

I have come a long way (cf. previous review, Wan 1982a) and been a long time in coming to greater appreciation of this volume: in the formats of pre-publication mimeograph and later in published book form (as key reference or textbook) for a period of about twenty years in teaching ministries, testing it out in three continents. Even this semester, I am using it as a text for my ethnohermeneutics class in the Doctor of Missiology Program at the Reformed Theological Seminary. I share the assessment of reviewer Robert L. Ramseyer:

> . . . a truly monumental attempt to show what cultural anthropology can do for our understanding of Christian faith and mission. As the most complete work in the field, *Christianity in Culture* is also the *best example* of the way in which our understanding of culture and the cultural process affects our understanding of Christian

# FIGURE 1 - THE BASICS OF KRAFT'S (1979a) MODEL

| CATEGORY | GENERAL PATTERN | KRAFT'S PREFERRED PATTERN |
|---|---|---|
| LANGUAGE (LINGUISTICS) | -sound, word, sentence, paragraph, etc.<br><br>-(phonology, morphology, syntax, semantics, etc.) | -variable in forms,<br>-efficient/impactful in function,<br>-constant in meaning<br><br>(4-7) |
| GOSPEL (EVANGELISM) | -the good news of salvation<br><br>-(multiple approaches: propositional, personal, presence, persuasion, program, power-encounter, etc.) | -meet the felt-need of receptor<br><br>-(various receptor-oriented means leading to the communication of the good news)<br><br>(8-12) |
| BIBLE (TRANSLATION) | -in different languages for different people-groups<br><br>-(formal-correspondence, dynamic -equivalence, etc.) | -choice of receptor-oriented types of translation of the Bible<br><br>-(dynamic-equivalence principle)<br><br>(13-17) |

**NOTE:** ( ) chapter numbering of Kraft's *Christianity in Culture*. (1979a) faith and life . . . especially helpful in this respect because the author is not afraid to *follow his anthropo- logical presuppositions to their obvious theological and missiological conclusions.* Where his predecessors were content to merely suggest, Kraft spells out in detail the *logical conclusions of consistently* acting on his understanding of society and culture . . . I felt strongly that this was at the same time both *the best book and the worst book* that I had read on this subject. I still feel that way (Ramseyer 1983:110, 115) *(emphasis mine).*

It is in the spirit of appreciation, at the invitation of Dr. Kraft's risk-taking, continuous searching, "open-minded development . . . dynamic and growing . . . you are free to disagree . . . are encouraged to join me in the quest for greater insight" (Kraft 1979a:xiii,12, 41; 1987b:139), within the context of friendly and frank discussion ("genuine dialog," Kraft 1987b:139) that the following comments are offered.

# FIGURE 2 - KRAFT'S INTER-DISCIPLINARY INTEGRATION

| SOURCE/ CATEGORY | EUGENE NIDA (K. PIKE, etc.) | | | | [NEO-ORTHODOXY and NEW HERMENEUTIC] | | | |
|---|---|---|---|---|---|---|---|---|
| | COMMUNICATION and SOCIAL SCIENCES | | | | [PHILOSOPHICAL and PRACTICAL THEOLOGY] | | | |
| | linguistic and communication sciences | | social/beh. sciences | | [existential theology, Bible translation, hermeneutics] | | [practical theology, missiology] | |
| DISCIPLINE | transformational grammar; and functional linguistics | communication theory and Bible translation | functional-ism; conceptual model and Christian model (2,3) | | [relational theology] (6) | [revelation and hermenuetics] (10-11) | evangelism | discipleship and church planting |
| BASIC IDEA | form, function, meaning (4,5) | three aspects: sender-message-receptor; communication with efficiency(8) | human commonality and worldview (5) | | [Incarnation (9) ethno-theology (7)] | [receptor-oriented understanding (12-13); ethnolinguistic interpretation(7)] | "be all..to all..by all means" (1Cor. 9) (cf.p.103,123, 128, 142,154,197, 230, 300,400) | [contextualization, trans-forming culture with God] (18,19) |
| KEY TERM | dynamic-equivalence (DE) / receptor-oriented (RO) | | | | | | | |
| | RO-principle/ DE-principle | RO-communication and DE-translation | [DE-transculturation (14)] | | [DE-theologizing (15)] | [RO-revelation(9) DE-translation of the inspired Casebook 13] | [DE-conversion (17) and DE-transculturation of the message (14)] | DE-churchness (16) |

NOTE: 1) ( ) chapter numbering in *Christianity in Culture*. (Kraft 1979a); 2) concepts and terms in [ ] are logical derivations of Kraft's consistent/coherent theoretical model; leaning towards theological deviation on Kraft's part from the evangelical position as represented by "The Chicago Statement on Biblical Hermeneutics" (Geisler 1978).

## KRAFT'S USE/MISUSE OF THE COMMUNICATION AND SOCIAL SCIENCES IN BIBLICAL INTERPRETATION AND MISSIOLOGICAL FORMULATION

Evangelical response to Kraft's ethnotheological model of integrating communication and social sciences with theology varied from positive (Buswell 1986, Saayman 1981), mixed (Adeney 1980, Conn 1984, Heselgrave 1992) to negative (Carson 1987 and 1993, Dryness 1980, Gross 1985, Heldenbrand 1982 and 1985, Henry 1980, Krass 1979, McQuilkin 1977, Scaer 1982, Wan 1982a). Two books have been published in response to Kraft's *Christianity in Culture*, i.e. Edward N. Gross's *Is Charles Kraft An Evangelical? A Critique of Christianity in Culture* (1985) of 100-plus pages and Harvie M. Conn's *Eternal Word and Chang-ing World* (1984) of 300-plus pages which was reviewed by Buswell (1986:71) who stated that "in many respects this work might be considered an extended . . . commentary on missionary anthro-pologist Charles Kraft's position developed mainly in his *Christianity in Culture*" (cf. Conn's own admission, 1984:330). Conn's review by far was the most fair and extensive appraisal of Kraft's model.

The following discussion is organized in the format of answers to four questions:

1) Has Kraft misused the communication and social sciences in his attempt of interdisciplinary integration? NO.
2) Has Kraft misused the communication and social sciences in his biblical interpretation and missiological formulation in light of his theoretical and methodological root being a linguist/communicologist? NO.
3) Has Kraft misused the communication and social sciences in his biblical interpretation from an evangelical perspective:
   –based on "The Willowbank Report" ? NO
   –based on "The Chicago Statement on Biblical Inerrancy"? YES
4) Has Kraft misused the communication and social sciences in his missiological formulation from an evangelical perspective:
   –based on "The Willowbank Report"? NO

–based on "The Chicago Statement on Biblical Inerrancy"?
YES

**Has Kraft misused the communication and social sciences in his attempt of interdisciplinary integration? NO.**

Kraft had been repeatedly commended for his insightful discussion on linguistic application to Bible translation (Adeney 1980, Conn 1984, Saayman 1981, Hesselgrave 1992, Ramseyer 1983) yet his critics faulted him either for his bad choice of an an-thropological theory called "functionalism" (Conn 1984, Remseyer 1983, Scaer 1982, Wan 1982a) or his non-evangelical theology in terms of "truth," "revelation," and "hermeneutics" (Carson 1987 and 1993, Conn 1978, Dryness 1980, Gross 1985, Heldenbrand 1982 and 1985, Henry 1980, Krass 1979, McQuilkin 1977 and 1980, Ramseyer 1983, Wan 1982a).

A careful study of Kraft's published works will show that his critics have misunderstood him very badly. In his writings, especially *Christianity in Culture*, he appears to be an anthropologist of the "functional" school and a theologian of "neo-orthodox" and "new hermeneutic" persuasion. He uses freely the terms and concepts of anthropological functionalism (e.g. "culture is an integrated system," "form and function," "equilibrium," "felt-need," "functional substitute," "efficiency," "impact," etc.); yet he never claims to be a "functionalist anthropologist." He employs with liberty the terms and concepts of scholars of "neo-orthodox" and "new hermeneutic" tradition (e.g. "continuous revelatory interaction between God and man," "revelation as a receptor-oriented communication," "the Bible as a case book of God's continuous dynamic interaction with man," "inspiration is an ongoing dynamic process of God's communication," etc.); he never identifies himself as a theologian. He is a linguist/ communicologist by self-profession (Kraft 1977:165; 1987:133; 1983) and by practice *par excellence*.

For instance, it is generally assumed by Kraft's theoretical friends (Buswell 1986, Conn 1984, Saayman 1981) and foes (Dyrness 1980, Helderbrand 1985, Ramseyer 1983, Wan 1982a) that his model of ethnotheology (Kraft 1979a) is based on his choice of functional anthropological theory (e.g. Conn 1984: chapter 3), traceable to the British (Malinowski, Radcliffe-Brown, etc.) and American (Franz Boas, Talcott Parsons, Robert Merton, etc.) traditions (cf. Buswell 1986, Hatch 1973, Harris 1968). This assumption of his personal choice of anthropological "functionalism" is not warranted by facts, i.e. his training, profession, publication and performance.

A diachronic analysis of the formation and development of Kraft's ethnotheological model began in linguistic/communi-cation sciences (Wan 1982a) and remains consistently as a com-munication model (Dyrness 1980:40). He began as a linguist by training (linguistics at Hartford Seminary Foundation), by research and profession (as a linguist/translator in the Hausa language of Nigeria), by publications (on Hausa: seven volumes between 1965-1973, thirteen articles between 1965-1976). Though not a member of the Summer Institute of Linguistics ("SIL" except in 1961-63, see Kraft 1987:133), he followed closely and "built upon" (Conn 1984:154-159) the foundation of SIL/ABS ("American Bible Society,") translators/linguists such as E. A. Nida, K. Pike, W. A. Smalley, W. D. Reyburn, J. A. Lowen, W. Wonderly, etc. (Conn 1984:154-159; Heldenbrand 1985:42).

It was not until Kraft's realization that his linguistic techniques and monocultural missionary training did not prepare and equip him to deal with cultural issues and contextualization problems (e.g. polygamy, spirits, Nigerian preference of the Old Testament to his beloved "Epistle to the Romans," etc.), that he was led to move into applied anthropology in research, reflection, and publication (Kraft 1979a: chapter 1). His model of ethnotheology in *Christianity in Culture* is a cumulative combination of linguistics/communication research (e.g. S-M-R, emic/etic and surface/deep analysis, functional linguistic, transformational grammar, receptor-orientation and dynamic-equivalence translation/communication, etc.) applied to anthropology, theology, with a strong dose of American pragmatism (e.g. efficiency, impact, practical "how-to," "functional fit," "felt-need," "receptor-orientation" for fruitful result, etc.). His ethnotheology has all the trappings of classical functionalism of European, and modern functionalism of contemporary American, cultural anthropology. At heart he is a linguist/communicologist and is busy at work (Kraft 1976c, 1977a, 1978c, 1979b, 1981, 1983 etc., see Appendix I) with the preoccupation of being efficient and im-pactful pragmatically (Wan 1982a). His call for being "personal" and "relational" (Kraft 1979a, 1983) is for the purpose of "good communication for good result" (Kraft 1979b, 1979e), or "ensuring the best return on the missionary investment" (Saayman 1981:90), a rather pragmatic and programmatic motivation that is "biblical" like the recruitment pattern of the scribes and Pharisees of the biblical time (Mt 23:15); but not "scriptural" (i.e. in obedience to God and with compassion to and love for the recipients, Mt 9:35-38; 28:18-20; etc.)

Kraft has achieved what he planned to do in *Christianity in Culture*, i.e. develop a "cross-cultural Christian theology" by integrating "anthropology, linguistics, translation theory, and communication science on areas of life and thought that have ordinarily been regarded as theological" (1979a:13). Credit is due him for his successful interdisciplinary integration with clarity, coherence, convincing presentation, etc. and for his momentous accomplishment (Ramseyer 1983:110). Even one of his strongest critics (100-plus pages of negative remarks) complemented him on this volume as "one of the most important books yet printed dealing with the current contextualization debate" (Gross 1985:3).

Kraft's model has been criticized by reviewer Ramseyer who said, "*Christianity in Culture* seems strangely unaware of confrontations and conflict in New Testament gospel sharing" (1983:112-113) on the basis of Kraft's "naive attempt to apply insight from one particular kind of cultural anthropology (static functionalism) to the Christian mission" (1983:115). Providentially, Kraft in 1984 experienced a "second paradigm shift" (cf. Kraft 1979a:6-12 being his first) which gave him a "kingdom perspective" with a "warfare mentality" realizing the reality of the spirit world. His "practice shift" (Kraft 1987:127) moving into the Christian deliverance ministries is theologically supported by his research and publication of several books: *Christianity with Pow-er* (1989), *Defeating Dark Angels* (1992), *Deep Wounds, Deep Healing* and *Behind Enemy Line* (both in 1994) and many articles.

Kraft began his research and writing in linguistics from 1963-1973, followed by his intensive study on and integration of anthropology, communication, translation, interpretation and contextualization in the 1970s with the resultant publication of *Christianity in Culture* in 1979. He then shifted his focus to the spirit world from the 1980s to the present. This pilgrimage of inter-disciplinary integration is similar to the wilderness experience of the Israelites due to his conception and

## 132 MISSIOLOGY AND THE SOCIAL SCIENCES

compartmentalization of reality, especially spiritual reality. Kraft took the "cultural/supracultural and absolute/relative" presupposition (epistemo-logical discussion here and theological critique later) from Nida with neither reservation nor modification (with reference to Nida in his 1979a "a total of 41 times," as observed by Conn, 1984:144). The weakness of Kraft's interdisciplinary approach lies in this faulty presupposition of reality (see Figure 3) in his theoretical formulation and the resultant research/ministry operation that took him many years of time and efforts moving from the lower

**FIGURE 3 - THE CULTURAL, SUPRACULTURAL, ABSOLUTE AND RELATIVE**
(Kraft 1979A:121)

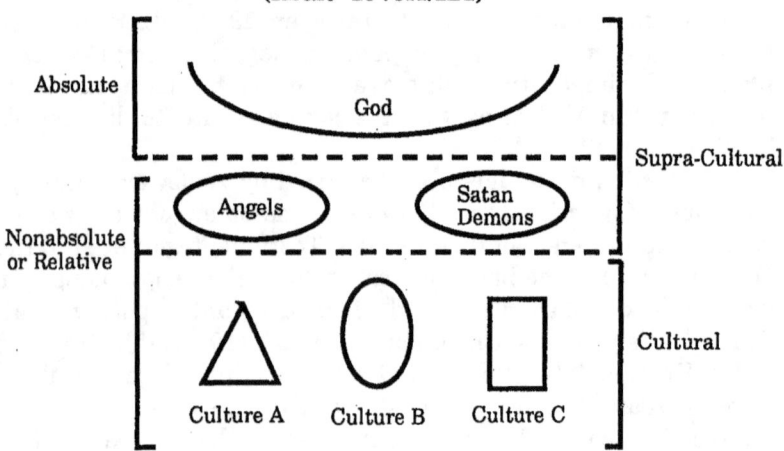

level (of functional linguistics) to the higher level (of "integrated culture," incarnation, inscripturation, interpretation of Scripture, ethnotheology) to the middle level (of angels, demons, deliverance ministries). Perhaps this is the problem Ramseyer (1983: 114) is trying to identify which "is a characteristic of the Western intellectual tradition . . . but his is unable to see that his attempts to split reality into principles and behavior, meaning and form . . . are the sort of Western intellectualizing which he warns his readers against." The following quotation may illustrate this point of duality conception and its correlated compartmentalizing operation:

The **dialectical logic** of the Ameri-European culture can best be understood in light of lineal conception of time and monochronic time-management . . . The extensive use of the Aristotelian logic, especially the law of identity and the law of contradiction . . . leads to a deep-rooted **perception of duality in reality and dialectical cognitive process in operation. It is axiomatic to categorize and classify everything in AE culture in terms of duality**: e.g. ethically right or wrong, good or bad; cosmologically nature or culture, temporal or eternal, the city of God or city of man, heaven or hell; cultural or supracultural, absolute or relative; existentially compartmentalize life into public or private, profession or personal, departmentalize . . . soteriologically the sovereignty of God or the free will of man; christologically the divine nature or human nature in the person of Christ, the historical Jesus or Christ of the **kerygma** (Wan 1982b, 1985); epistemologically true or false; aesthetically beautiful or ugly, etc. The list of **duality** can be easily multiplied (Wan 1995:15)

A new definition and concept of "culture" is proposed as an alternative that would not presuppose humanity as a "closed system" (Wan 1982b), compartmentalized from angelic beings and the Divine Being (the Three Persons of the Triune God). This new model of reality will enable evangelical Christians to develop a "symphonic integration" that is multi-disciplinary (not just a "trialogue" of anthropology, missiology and theology as proposed by Conn 1984), multi-contextual (Wan 1982b, 1994), multi-dimensional (Holmes 1983), and multi-perspectival (Conn 1984:335-337, Poythress 1987). (See Appendix II—*A Symphonic Approach to Interdisciplinary Integration: A Vari-dynamic Mod-el*. This "vari-dynamic model" is to be "Trinitarian" in theology and epistemology, "incarnational" in anthropology and method-ology, "contextual-interactional" in contextualization, multi-dimensional and interdisciplinary in demonology and deliverance ministries, family-focussed in the practice of evangelism, discipleship, church planting, ethnohermeneutically in theologizing which is biblically based, scripturally sound and culturally sensitive, see Wan 1982b, 1985, 1988, 1989, 1990, 1991a, 1991b, 1994, 1995).

**Has Kraft misused the communication and social sciences in his biblical interpretation and missiological formulation in light of his theoretical and methodological root being a linguist/commu-nicologist? NO.**

If one criticizes Kraft's ethnotheology from an anthropological perspective (as I did in 1982) one is overlooking his strength in consistent and creative, insightful and innovative interdisciplinary integration (see previous quote of Ramseyer, 1984). Attacking Kraft's view on "truth," "revelation," "interpre-tation," etc. as presented in *Christianity in Culture* theologically without considering his theoretical and methodological base in linguistic and communication sciences, as did many of his critics (e.g. Carson 1987 and 1993, Conn 1978, Dryness 1980, Gross 1985, Heldenbrand 1982 and 1985, Henry 1980, Krass 1979, McQuilkin 1977 and 1980, Ramseyer 1983, Wan 1982a) is indeed a real mistake. Kraft has neither the intention nor the pretention to declare himself a theologian (whether it be an "evangelical" one or not is beside the point). On one occasion he expressed his frustration at being misunderstood, "it is unlikely that a 'med-dler' (of theology) like myself could function competently as a theologian" (Kraft 1977:166).

He, (by confession "academically I am labeled an anthropological linguist," Kraft 1977:165) is a linguist/communicologist /missiologist busying himself in his courageous venture into the hinterland of "cross-cultural theologizing" (sub-title of 1979a) *dynamically* (to be different from the traditional "static" approach, 1979a:32-38), *"open-mindedly"* (to break away from the "closed-minded conservative," 1979a:39-41), *cross-culturally* (to swim against the current of mono-cultural theologizing of the regular practice of western theologians, Kraft 1979a: chapter 7), *contextually* (to avoid the pitfall of the old-fashioned "cultural imperialist"), *progressively* (termed "cumulative revelation information" of the Bible rather than "progressive revelation" of the closed-minded evangelical, Kraft 1979a: chapters 9-12), *pragmatically* (for "efficiency" and "impact"), *communicatively* (see Figure 3). His strength in being theoretically consistent and coherent has misled him theologically (see [ ] items on the right side of Figure 2).

Kraft is to be praised for his courage to go beyond his linguist/comminicologist predecessors, Nida, Pike, Smalley, Wonderly, etc. (cf. quote of Ramseyer 1983 previously), embarking on his journey of interdisciplinary integration of "cross-cultural theologizing" by way of communication (Kraft 1973d, 1974a, 1980, 1983), psychology (Kraft 1974b, 1986), anthropology (Kraft 1975, 1977, 1978b, 1980, 1985), theology (Kraft 1972a, 1972b, 1979a) and missiology (Kraft 1978a, 1978b). In *Christianity in Culture*, Kraft is charting a new path of multidisciplinary integration and in the process he might have controversially attracted criticism on his theology by the well-intentioned "defenders" of the evangelical faith in the persons of Harvey Conn (1978), William Dyrness (1980), Edward Gross (1985), Carl Henry (1980), Richard Heldenbrand (1982 and 1985), and Robertson McQuilkin (1977 and 1980). Only a linguist/communicologist would be eager to develop a new "theology of communication" and make "biblical" but not "scriptural" statements as listed in Figure 4.

Kraft's best contribution to interdisciplinary integration is his insightful analysis of language, translation, communication and his masterful synthetic model of communication. Even his critics complement him: "[Kraft] has produced a book which contains a wealth of extremely helpful ideas and suggestions. He is at his best when he discusses language. Chapter 13 on the translation of the Bible is excellent" (Ramseyer 1983:115).

## FIGURE 4 - KRAFT'S (1983)
## THEOLOGY OF COMMUNICATION

| COMMUNICATION THEOLOGY (Kraft's theological assumptions) | COMMUNICATION THEORY (Kraft's interdiscipline integration) |
|---|---|
| God:<br>-the REALITY, Originator of principle (215)<br>-God's communication goal: personal relationship with man (20-22)<br>-the MESSAGE of communication (58, 207) | Assumption:<br>-"God abides by the communicational rules he built into his creation"; therefore "we can and should imitate God's example" (215)<br>-critical realism (223) |
| the Incarnation: (23-26)<br><br>-identificational communication (15) | we learn from Jesus: (23-25)<br>-personal participation in the lives of his receptors;<br>-love = primary concern for receptor<br>-respects, trusts and makes himself dependent on and vulnerable to receptor |
| the Bible:<br>=record of the revelation of God's message (215)<br>=manual/case-book of communication (16)<br>=precedents and principles of communication (16)<br>=inspiration of message extends to method (3) | communicator should:<br>-adopt the receptor's frame of reference (culture, language, etc.) (41);<br>-have relational and specific message (21) |
| "truth":<br>-meaning determined by receptor (89-108)<br>-relativity, receptor-dependence (109-113) | message: (75-82)<br>-interaction, multiple, irretrievable, complex, 6 types |
| hermeneutics: (189-190)<br>-interpreting the Bible = communication<br>-interpreting the "truth" (interpretational reflex) | meaning exists: (109-133)<br>-neither objectively (external) nor subjectively (in symbols);<br>-is result of interpretation; thus receptor-dependent and is relative |

| | |
|---|---|
| the Gospel: life-changing message of the Great Commission (i.e. communicating the good news throughout the world")(17) | Jesus is the master/effective communicator: (22-34, 195-207)<br>-7 things to learn: 1) segment audience; 2) enter receptor's frame of reference;<br>3) control vehicles; 4) self + message; 5) credible; 6) relevant; 7) specific |
| evangelism and Bible translation:<br>-communicating for life-change (222);<br>-the person as medium (160);<br>-translation as communication (171) | -10 myths of communication (35-54)<br>-3 factors of communication: (64-75) goal, audience, method of presentation |
| -conversion: -"paradigm shift" (radical change of perspective) (271)<br>-church planting: dynamic equivalence Christian group | -receptors have needs (9);<br>-7 stages of receptor's decision-making (105) |
| -effective communication for deep-level change: worldview, value, commitment (221-224)<br>-dynamic communication with efficiency and impact (48, 82-88, 238-240) ||

**NOTE:** ( ) page numbering in *Communication Theory for Christian Witness* (1983)

**Has Kraft misused the communication and social sciences in his biblical interpretation from an evangelical perspective:**
**- based on "The Willowbank Report" ? NO**
**- based on "The Chicago Statement on Biblical Inerrancy"? YES**

Dr. Kraft was one of the dozens of participants and presenters (Kraft 1980b) at the Consultation on Gospel and Culture held at Willowbank, Somerset Bridge, Bermuda from 6th to 13th January 1978, sponsored by the Lausanne Theology and Education Group. "The Willowbank Report" was published (Coote and Stott 1980:308-342) as the result of the gathering. His input at the consultation and the drafting of "The Willowbank Report" could be identified and there is *no* apparent *conflict* between that report and his ethnotheological model.

However, implicit in Kraft's model of ethnotheology in terms of *biblical interpretation* are two assumptions that are *in conflict* with "The Chicago Statement on Biblical Inerrancy": i.e. his epistemological assumption is in conflict with Article III and his methodological assumption with Article V.

Firstly, in his reaction against the rationalist's (like Carl Henry or Harold Lindsell) insistence on "propositional/objective truth" to be "static" and his avoidance of neo-orthodox's (like Barth and Thiselton) "subjective truth," he opted for Ian Barbour's (1974) "critical realism" for the sake of being theoretically consistent to arrive at a "relational truth" (Walters 1982) which Kraft described as "receptor-oriented" understanding of truth (Kraft 1979a). The Bible being "God's revelational information" is only "potential revelation" until the recipient's proper understanding/interpreting to have the "meaning" (with the Holy Spirit as the activator). This is at variance with Article III of "The Chicago Statement," which states that "[w]e deny the Bible is merely a witness to revelation, or only becomes revelation in encounter, or depends on the responses of men for its validity" (Geisler 1980:494-495). John Dahms added to A. Holmes' (1977:34-38) two-dimensional understanding of "truth" to be three: "in biblical usage truth is sometimes a quality of propositions, sometimes a quality of persons and things (especially a characteristic of ultimate reality), and sometimes a quality of conduct or action" (Dahms 1994:8). And the "unity of truth" is to be found in the Logos– the Word– Incarnated and inscripturated. See Appendix IV for the multi-dimensional, multi-level, multi-contextual understanding of God's revelation that would allow a "symphonic multi-disciplinary integration" under the direction of the Triune God (i.e. the Father likened to the composer, the Son the music/theme and the Holy Spirit the conductor, using the same score—the Word Incarnate and inscripturated.)

Secondly, Kraft's ethnotheology model has a methodological assumption that is *not in accordance* with Article V of "The Chicago Statement": "God's revelation in the Holy Scriptures was progressive . . . deny that any normative revelation has been given since the completion of the New Testament writings" (Geisler 1980:495). Kraft's model is built on the "synchronic" dimension of "functional linguistics" and "transformational grammar" which would lead him to be devoid of the historical dimension of the Bible in his interpretation (e.g. "progressive revelation" and the Christian faith, e.g. Israel and the New Testament church as God's covenant people, see Conn 1974:4; Dyrness 1980:40). His extensive, almost exclusive, use of the communication model and the emphasis on God's "dynamic continuous interaction") with humanity would have similar effects of denying the closed "canon" of the Bible historically and thus confusing "inspiration" with "illumination," see Appendix III. Here are examples of Kraft's "unscriptural" statements:

> God has inspired and still inspires (Kraft 1979a: 205; 1987:126).

> Yet in many ways tradition ('law'), tribe and ceremony in Hebrew culture were the functional equivalents of grace, freedom, and philosophizing in Greek culture. The latter are not necessarily superior ways of expressing the Gospel, just different culturally (Kraft 1979a: 232).

> Yet I had concluded that a living God is a still revealing God (Kraft 1987:126).

The historicity and historical dimension of the Christian faith cannot and should not be lost by the undiscriminatory adoption of a mere synchronic/communicational/dynamic-interaction model of "time-zero" for the sake of emic-based understanding of "meaning" or efficient communication with impact, because these have ill-effects on his interpretation of the Bible and cross-cultural theologizing. Kraft's "unscriptural" statements of Figure 2 (in [ ]) warrant some comments here. God is not just the "MESSAGE" of Christian communication (Kraft 1979a:chapter 9; 1983:58, 207). Jesus, the Incarnate Word is not just the "master/effective communicator" (Kraft 1979a:chapter 6; 1983:23-34, 195-207; see Figure 1 and Figure 2). If "Jesus of Nazareth" (termed "form" in Kraft's model to be considered "relative") should be separated from the"Christ of *kerygma*" (termed "meaning" in Kraft's model to be "recepter-oriented/determined") as Kraft has done (e.g. "word/form" separated from "meaning" in linguistics and from "meaning/message" in communication) then this Christology of Kraft is no longer evangelical and this type of interdisciplinary integration (of linguistic and communication sciences with theology) is improper. The Bible, the inscripturated

Word, is neither just the "the measure of revelation" nor just "the record of the revelational information from God," nor the "manual/case-book of communication" (Kraft 1979a:187-190; 1983:16, 215, see Appendix V). Carson (1977) criticized Kraft's view of the Bible "as a casebook" and made some strong statements:

> He treats the Bible as a casebook, in which different narratives or passages might reasonably be applied to one particular culture but not to another ... it appears as if Kraft's reliance on contemporary hermeneutics has simultaneously gone too far and not far enough. He has gone too far in that by treating the Bible as a casebook he does not ask how the pieces fit together. Indeed, he necessarily assumes that they do not ... But he does not go far enough in that he fails to recognize that even basic statements such as "Jesus is Lord" are in certain respects culturally conditioned ... "Jesus" is not an entirely unambiguous proper noun; are we referring to the Jesus of the Mormons, the Jesus of the Jehovah's Witnesses, the Jesus of liberal Protestantism ... of orthodox Christianity (Carson 1993:58-59)

Kraft's use of the Bible to formulate his "theology of communication" and his application of the RO-/DE-principle in hermeneutics and cross-cultural theologizing is a violation of the general teaching (termed "plain meaning" or not being in "functional control of the Bible" by McQuilkin 1980). In simple terms, Kraft's biblical interpretation and missiological formulation is "biblical" but not "scriptural."

Since God's revelation and our interpretation have multi-dimensional, multi-level, multi-contextual complexity, evangelical interpretation and cross-cultural theologizing (Conn 1978:44-45; Wan 1994) should not only be "biblical" but also "scriptural," not individualistic but communal and complex ("convenantal community" in Conn 1984:231-235; "complexity and necessity" in Wan 1994; see Appendix VI and Figure 5 below).

## FIGURE 5—THE REVELATORY and HERMENEUTICAL CIRCLE

revelatory process    A = Bible Author (the Triune God)
--->    --->             B = Bible Writers (Moses to Apostle John)
A    B    C or D     C = Christian recipients/ Interpreter / communicator
<---   <---           D = Non-Christian Recipients/Interpreter
hermeneutical process

As one evangelical anthropologist observed, "Kraft has opened himself up to the charge of being too beholden to the 'God of culture' and a 'high view of culture/low view of scripture'." (Hesselgrave 1991:129).

**Has Kraft misused the communication and social sciences in his missiological formulation from an evangelical perspective:**
- **based on "The Willowbank Report"? NO**
- **based on "The Chicago Statement on Biblical Inerrancy"? YES**

Kraft *has not misused* the communication and social sciences in his *missiological formulation,* from an evangelical perspective based on "The Willowbank Report," but *did so* if examined on the basis of "The Chicago Statement on Biblical Inerrancy." Implicit in his model of ethnotheology are two questionable assumptions: anthropological assumption cf. Article XIV and methodological assumption cf. Article XVIII.

In contemporary linguistic science, language is considered axiomatically to be "an arbitrary system for communication" that is relative in value and morally neutral. Kraft (following Nida, Pike, etc.) made use of the translation/communication model (i.e. the RO- and DE-principle, see Figure 2) and extensively applied it to transculturation, cross-cultural theologizing and evangelism, etc. The anthropological assumption is that "culture is analogous to language in that the relationship between cultural forms and the meanings which they convey is essentially arbitrary" (Ramseyer 1983:111). Evangelical Christian anthropologists can neither assume "culture" to be morally neutral, presupposing it to be relative in value (i.e. human cultures approximate the "scriptural" standing in varying degrees), nor merely arbitrary (i.e. the image of

God, the fallenness of humanity, the transforming power of the gospel, etc., cf. reviewers: Adeney 1980:26; Henry 1980:157; Ramseyer 1983:110). The importance of the New Testament epistles in terms of fulfillment of the Old Testament books is based on the assumption of "the unity and internal consistency of Scripture" (Article XIV) and is not due to the cultural preference of monocultural Western missionaries and could not be opted out by any cultural groups because of cultural affinity to or preference for portions of the Bible (Kraft 1979a:chapters 13-15; cf. Carson 1987 and 1993).

"We affirm that the text of Scripture . . . den[ies] the legitimacy of any treatment of the text or quest for sources lying behind it that leads to relativizing, dehistoricizing or discounting its teaching" is affirmed by "The Chicago Statement" (Article XVIII). It is at variance with Kraft's methodological assumption which is communication-reductionist and instrument-teleological.

The term "communication" used by Kraft is frequent and fluid. For a communicologist like Kraft, everything is "communication." Yet Kraft provided no specific definition of the term "communication" in either 1979a or 1983; the closest one of such is as follows:

> The use of the terms *preach* and *proclaim* as virtually the only translations of *kerusso* and several other Greek terms suggest . . . In present day English, at least, such a term is readily at hand in the word *communicate*. I would, therefore, contend that the broad presentation of the gospel is intended by such Greek terms as *kerusso*, it would be more accurate to translate it "communicate (Kraft 19783:43).

Subsequently, Kraft can include everything under the term "communicate." According to Kraft's theology of communication (see Figure 4): "God is the MESSAGE of communication," "the Incarnation is identification communication," translating and interpreting the Bible is "communicate," etc. Thus "communicate" is a catch-all generic label (from God's inspiration, redemption, and salvation to the Christian's evangelism, theologizing, and church planting) that is so broad, so vague, so inclusive, etc. that it would confuse those who seek to communicate effectively and impactfully to use the term "communication" more carefully.

Kraft's communication-reductionist model of the "RO-/DE-principle" (see Figure 2) has a methodological assumption that evangelical Christians would question, including his methodology statement, "the inspirtation of the Bible extends both to the message and the method" (Kraft 1983:3). Reviewer Ramseyer sounded the alarm:

> In far too many cases, however, it has been assumed that the gospel is simply a message to be communicated and that whatever these sciences tell us about the communication of messages can be used to facilitate the communication of the gospel (Ramseyer 1983:108)

The gospel is not like any "message." Evangelism is not like any communication (McQuilkin 1977:40-41). Conversion is not just "paradigm shift." The Incarnation is not just "identification communication." There are the divine dimension, the spiritual reality, the theo-dynamic and angel-dynamic contexts (see Figure 6). In all the examples listed above, "communication" is only "the necessary but not sufficient" factor and is only one dimension of reality. To be communication-reductionistic is to be simplistic in theory, "biblical" but not "scriptural" (see Appendix IV to Appendix VI), just communicational without commitment in "heart" and "life" (see Conn 1978:43 for discussion on John Calvin's *theologia pietatis* of covenant witness with covenant life).

The methodological assumption in terms of instrumental/teleological presupposition/preoccupation (Wan 1994) is a serious problem from an evangelical perspective. Conn (1978:42; 1984:192-205) wrongly identified McGavran's attempt to reduce the gospel to a "core" of threefold affirmations for evangelization as the result of Cartesian rationalism and stated that "the simple gospel is never that simple." (A better option is to have a "center set" of approach that is theo-dynamic, Christocentric, scripturally sound and culturally sensitive, Wan 1982b, 1994). Kraft's model of ethnotheology shared the same instrumental/teleological presupposition/preoccupation with success, efficiency and impact. (Even more alarming is the "functional Trinitrian" view of God embraced by both Nida (1959a:53) and Kraft (1979a:195). This would explain his readiness to propose his felt-need, non-combative, receptor-oriented approach for "minimal dislocation," and maximum efficiency in his contextualized Muslim evangelism (Conn 1984:192-195; Heldenbrand 1982, 1985; Kraft 1982b; McQuilkin 1977:40) (See Figure 6).

For evangelicals the gospel is "the power of God unto salvation" (Ro 1:16-17) and theo-dynamic. Evangelism is different from other kinds of communication; similar to incarnation, inscripturation, illumination for it is theo-dynamic in nature, Christo-centric, multi-contextual, multi-dimensional, multi-individual (the Triune God, the Bible-writer, the human messenger/evangelist, the receptor, etc see Appendix IV and Appendix V). It is not human-centered, not merely message/meaning/means-based, not receptor-dependent alone, not outcome-determined. In Christianity, "the means" and "the messenger," are also determined by the "message" of God-revealing truth, God-redeeming power, and in a God-character way. Following Nida's lead on "supracultural/cultural, absolute/relative" principle, Kraft credited God with being the only "absolute"; everything else is relative, cultural, functional, adaptable, etc. was for the purpose of building a biblical basis for his pragmatic/functional/relative/teleological way of theoretical formulation and missiological application.

"Scripturally" speaking, evangelism is not just a Christian's effort to minimize the negative elements of the gospel to "market it" for effective membership recruitment for a "Christian club." It is a divinely motivated/enabled/guided Christian's effort to make committed disciples (not just communicating the gospel message to appeal to the "felt-need" of the receptive recipient) whose transformed lives should be nurtured in the Christian fellowship of the church—an organism, not a social aggregate of individuals with "paradigm shift."

However, Kraft's most recent "paradigm shift" 1989:82-85) and "practice shift" (1987:127) have shown a very healthy and scriptural shift from this methodological presupposition and preoccuptaion with "gospel-marketing," receptor's felt need, consumer orientation for success, efficiency, etc. His articles (1986a, 1987b, 1991, 1992) have repeatedly emphasized "allegiance encounter," and "truth encounter" (as suggested by

# FIGURE 6 - WAN'S ANALYSIS OF KRAFT'S (1983) MODEL

| KRAFT'S MODEL | | WAN'S ANALYSIS | |
|---|---|---|---|
| COMMUNICATION PATTERN | COMMUNICATION CATEGORY | CHRISTIAN EQUIVALENCE | MISSING ELEMENT |
| know and master the principle of: form, function, and meaning | surface level: multiplicity of form and function | understanding the Scripture; personal evangelism | inspiration: Bible = divine-human Book evangelism/illumination: divine-human interaction |
| receptor-oriented communication | deep-level: paradigm-shift | spiritual repentance and conversion | kernel level: personal interaction (like human sexual intimacy) |
| communication with efficiency and impact | goal-oriented communication | spiritual reality of being born-again | deep level: spiritual regeneration (like amalgamation with genetic pooling |
| DE-Christian group | successful and efficient communication | discipleship and church planting | transformed life, committed disciple, organismic church with body-life |

reviewers Conn 1984:229-235; Ramseyer 1983:112) in addition to the popular understanding or "power encounter," thanks to his former colleague Paul Hiebert (for Kraft's recognition, see 1992:215). And his books (1989, 1992, 1994a 1994b) have included the confrontational, conflicting, combattive elements of the gospel and evangelism (as suggested by reviewer Ramseyer 1983:112-113). Better yet, the Trinity is involved (as suggested by reviewers Conn 1974:45, 1984231; Dyrness 1980:40; Henry 1980:163; Wan 1982b) at every stage of encounter with a sound "scriptural" foundation for "power encounter" (1992:217), "allegiance encounter" and "truth encounter" (1992:218). This is a full circle, of going from the study of homino-culture (e.g. from linguistic and communication sciences to social sciences) to theo-culture (e.g. inspiration, incarnation, etc.), to angel-culture (e.g. power-encounter) and back to homino-culture. There is evidence of a holistic view of humanity (with the multi-dimension of cognition, volition and affection), a balanced view of human culture, a scriptural understanding of reality, a non-dualistic and non-dychotomistic frame of reference, and non-reductionistic approach to ministry (Wan 1988, 1989, 1991b, 1995).

## CONCLUSION

In this study, Kraft's contribution to inter-disciplinary integration by using the communication and social sciences has been analyzed and recognized. His use/misuse of the communication and social sciences in biblical interpretation and missiological formulation have been examined and critiqued. A new concept and definition of "culture" has been proposed as a constructive suggestion for the improvement of Kraft's theoretical and theological (evangelical) approach. This new "vari-dynamic model" will lead to a "symphonic approach" (not just dialogue or trialogue) of multi-disciplinary, multi-level, multi-contextual, multi-dimensional integration. Kraft's recent shift from reductionistic, non-dychotomistic, non-evangelical and "unscriptur-al" approachs of inter-disciplinary integration is most encouraging.

It is high time for Dr. Kraft to revise his influential yet controversial book *Christianity in Culture* (1979a) incorporating his new insights and recent discoveries, as a contribution to evangelical scholarship in interdisciplinary integration.

## REFERENCE LIST

Adeney, Miriam

    1980    Christianity in Culture. *Radix* 2 (Jan/Feb): 25-26.

Barney, G. Linwood

    1973    "The Supracultural and the Cultural: Implications for Frontier Missions." In *The Gospel and Frontier Peoples: A Report of a Consultation*, Dec. 1972, edited by R. Pierce Beaver. Pp. 48-57. Pasadena, CA: William Carey Library.

Berkhof, L.

    1969    *Principles of Biblical Interpretation*. Grand Rapids, MI: Baker Book House.

Buswell, James O., III

    1986    "Conn on Functionalism and Presupposition in Missionary Anthropology [review article]." *Trinity Journal* 7: 69-95.

Carson, Donald A.

    1987    "Church and Mission: Reflections on Contextualization and the Third Horizon." In *The Church in the Bible and the World: An International Study*. Edited by D. A. Carson. Pp. 213-257. Grand Rapids, MI: Baker Book House.

    1993    "Christian Witness in an Age of Pluralism." In *God and Culture*. Edited by D. A. Carson and John D. Woodbridge. Pp. 31-66. Grand Rapids, MI: William B. Eerdmans Publishing Company.

Cohen, Percy S.

    1968    *Modern Social Theory*. New York: Baadic Books, Inc.

Conn, Harvie M.

1978  "Contextualization: A New Dimension for Cross-Cultural Hermeneutic." *Evangelical Missions Quarterly* 14(1): 39-46.

1984  *Eternal Word and Changing Worlds: Theology, Anthropology and Mission in Trialogue.* Grand Rapids: Zondervan Publishing House.

Coote, Rober T. and John Stott, eds.

1980  *Down to Earth: Studies in Christianity and Culture—The Papers of the Lausanne Consultation on Gospel and Culture.* Grand Rapids, MI: William B. Eerdmans Publishing Company.

Dahms, John V.

1995  "The Biblical Concept of Truth." Unpublished paper. Canada: Canadian Theological Seminary.

Dyrness, William A.

1980  "Putting the Truth in Human Terms." *Christianity Today* 24 (April): 515-516.

Geisler, Norman L.

1980  *Inerrancy.* Grand Rapids, MI: Zondervan Publishing House.

Gross, Edward N.

1985  *Is Charles Kraft An Evangelical? A Critique of Christianity in Culture.* Elkins Park, PA: Christian Beacon Press.

Harris, Marvin

1968  *The Rise of Anthropological Theory.* New York: Thomas Y. Crowell Co.

Hatch, Elvin

1973  *Theories of Man and Culture.* New York: Columbia University Press.

Heldenbrand, Richard

1982  "Missions to Muslims: Cutting the Nerve?" *Evangelical Missions Quarterly* 18(3, July): 134-139.

1985 *Current Issues in Foreign Missions.* Warsaw, IN: Ministry to Muslims Project.

Henry, Carl F. H.

    1980 "The Cultural Relativizing of Revelation." *Trinity Journal* 1 (Fall): 153-64.

Hesselgrave, David J.

    1991 *Communicating Christ Cross-Culturally.* Grand Rapids: Zondervan Publishing House.

Holmes, Arthur F.

    1977 *All Truth is God's Truth.* Grand Rapids, MI: William B. Eerdmans Publishing Company.

    1983 *Contours of a World view.* Grand Rapids, MI: William B. Eerdmans Publishing Company.

Krass, Alfred C.

    1979 "Contextualization for Today." *Gospel in Context* 2(3, July): 27-30.

McQuilkin, J. Robertson

    1977 "The Behavioral Sciences Under the Authority of Scripture." *Journal of the Evangelical Theological Society* 20(1, March): 31-43.

    1980 "Limits of Cultural Interpretation." *Journal of the Evangelical Theological Society* 23(2, June): 113-124.

Nida, Eugene

    1959 "Are We Really Monotheist?" *Practical Anthropology* 6: 49-54.

    1971 "New Religions for Old: A Study of Culture Change in Religion." *Church and Culture Change in Africa.* Edited by David J. Bosch. Pretoria: N.G. Kerkbockhandel.

Poythress, Vern Sheridan

    1987    *Symphonic Theology: The Validity of Multiple Perspectives in Theology.* Grand Rapids, MI: Zondervan Publishing House.

Ramseyer, Robert L.

    1983    "Christian Mission and Cultural Anthropology." In *Exploring Church Growth.* Edited by Wilbert Shenk. Grand Rapids, MI: William Eerdmans Publishing Company.

Saayman, Willem

    1981    Review of *Christianity in Culture* by Charles H. Kraft. *Missionalia* 9(1, April): 89-90.

Scaer, David

    1982    "Functionalism Fails the Test of Orthodoxy." *Christianity Today* (February): 90.

Shenk, Wilbert R., ed.

    1983    *Exploring Church Growth.* Grand Rapids, MI: William B. Eerdmans Publishing Company.

Wan, Enoch

    1982a    "Critique of Functional Missionary Anthropology." *His Dominion* (Canadian Theological Seminary) 8(3, April).

    1982b    "The Theological Application of the Contextual Interaction Model of Culture."*His Dominion* (Canadian Theological Seminary) 9(1, October).

    1985    "Tao—The Chinese Theology of God-Man." *His Dominion* (Canadian Theological Seminary), Spring, 24-27.

    1988    "Spiritual Warfare: Understanding Demonization." *Alliance Family* (Manila, Philippines: CAMACOP), Summer, 6-18.

    1989    "Deliverance from Demonization." *Alliance Family* (Manila, Philippines: CAMACOP), Spring, 8-12.

1990 "Ethnic Receptivity Factors and Evangelism." In *Reclaiming A Nation*. Edited by Arnell Motz. Richmond, BC: Church Leadership Library. Pp.117-132.

1991a "The Theology of Family: A Chinese Case Study of Contextualization." *Chinese in North America*, March - April.

1991b "The Theology of Spiritual Formation: A Case Study of Contextualized Chinese Theology." *Chinese in North America*, March-April, 2-7.

1994 "Ethnohermenutics: Its Necessity and Difficulty for All Christians of All Times." Unpublished paper presented at the Evangelical Theological Society, Chicago, IL, November 1994.

1995 "Horizon of Inter-philosophical Dialogue: A Paradigmatic Comparative Study of the Ameri-European and The Sino-Asian Cognitive Patterns/Processes." Unpublished paper presented at the Second Symposium of Chinese-Western Philosophy and Religious Studies, October 4-6, 1995, Beijing, China.

Wolters, Al

1982 "Truth as Relational." *Theological Forum* 9(3 and 4): 7-11.

# APPENDIX I: PARTIAL BIBLIOGRAPHY OF CHARLES H. KRAFT

*Books*

1963 *A Study of Hausa Syntax* (3 vols.). Hartford Studies in Linguistics, vols. 8, 9, 10.

1965 *An Introduction to Spoken Hausa* (textbook, workbook, tapes). African Language Monographs 5A, 5B. African Studies Center: Michigan State University.

1966a  *Cultural Materials in Hausa.* African Language Monograph 6A. African Studies Center: Michigan State University.

1966b  *Workbook in Intermediate and Advanced Hausa.* African Language Monograph 6B. African Studies Center: Michigan State University.

1966c  *Where Do I Go From Here?* (A Handbook for Continuing Language Study in the Field), with Marguerite G. Kraft. U.S. Peace Corps.

1973a  *Teach Yourself Hausa*, with A. H. M. Kirk-Greene. English Universities Press.

1973b  *Introductory Hausa*, with M. G. Kraft. University of California Press.

1973c  *Hausa Reader.* University of California Press.

1979a  *Christianity in Culture.* Maryknoll, NY: Orbis Books.

1979b  *Communicating the Gospel God's Way.* Pasadena,CA: William Carey Library.

1979c  *Readings in Dynamic Indigeneity*, with T. Wisley. Pasadena, CA: William Carey Library.

1981  *Chadic Wordlists* (3 vols.). Berlin: Verlag von Dietrich Reimer.

1983  *Communication Theory for Christian Witness.* Nashville: Abingdon Press.

1989  *Christianity with Power.* Ann Arbor, MI: Servant Books.

1992  *Defeating Dark Angels.* Ann Arbor, MI: Servant Books.

1994a  *Deep Wounds, Deep Healing.* Ann Arbor, MI: Servant Books.

1994b  *Behind Enemy Lines*, edited. Ann Arbor, MI: Servant Books.

*Articles, Editorials and Chapters in Books*

1963 "Christian Conversion or Cultural Conversion?" *Practical Anthropology* 10: 179-187.

1964 "A New Study of Hausa Syntax." *Journal of African Languages* 3: 66-74.

1969 "What You Heard is Not What I Meant." *World Vision* Magazine 13: 10-12. (Reprinted in *Messenger* 118(16, 1969): 20-22.)

1971a "The New Wine of Independence." *World Vision* 15(2, February): 6-9.

1971b "Younger Churches—Missionaries and Indigeneity." *Church Growth Bulletin* 7: 159-61.

1972a "Theology and Theologies I." *Theology, News and Notes* 18(2, June): 4-6, 9.

1972b "Spinoff From the Study of Cross-Cultural Mission." *Theology, News and Notes* 18(3, October): 20-23.

1972c "The Hutterites and Today's Church." *Theology, News and Notes* 18(3, October): 15-16.

1972d "Theology and Theologies II." *Theology, News and Notes* 18(3, October): 17-20.

1973a "Toward a Christian Ethnotheology." In *God, Man and Church Growth*, edited by A. R. Tippett. Pp. 109-26. Grand Rapids, MI: William B. Eerdmans Publishing Company.

1973b "Church Planters and Ethnolinguistics." In *God, Man and Church Growth*, edited by A. R. Tippett. Pp. 226-49. Grand Rapids, MI: William B. Eerdmans Publishing Company.

1973c "God's Model for Cross-Cultural Communication—The Incarnation." *Evangelical Missions Quarterly* 9: 205-16.

1973d "The Incarnation, Cross-Cultural Communication—The Incarnation." *Evangelical Missions Quarterly* 9: 277-84.

1973e "Dynamic Equivalence Churches." *Missiology* 1(October): 39-57. Reprinted in *Readings in Dynamic Indigeneity,* edited by C. H. Kraft and T. N. Wisley. Pp. 87-111. Pasadena: William Carey Library.

1973f "North America's Cultural Heritage." *Christianity Today* 17(8, January 19): 6-8.

1974a "Ideological Factors in Intercultural Communication." *Missiology* 2: 295-312.

1974b "An Anthropologist's Response to Oden." In *After Therapy What?* edited by Neil C. Warren. Pp. 136-59. Springfield, IL: Charles C. Thomas.

1975 "Toward an Ethnography of Hausa Riddling." *Ba Shiru* 6: 17-24.

1976a "Communicate or Compete?" *Spectrum* (Spring-Summer): 8-10.

1976b "Cultural Concommitants of Higi Conversion: Early Periods." *Missiology* 4: 431-42.

1976c "Inter-cultural Communication and Worldview Change." Unpublished paper, School of World Mission, Pasadena, CA.

1977a "Biblical Principles of Communication." *The Harvester* 56: 262-64, 275. Edited and reprinted in *Buzz* (December, 1977), New Malden, Surrey, pp. 17, 19.

1977b "Can Anthropological Insight Assist Evangelical Theology?" *Christian Scholar's Review* 7: 165-202.

1978a "The Contextualization of Theology." *Evangelical Missions Quarterly* 14: 311-36.

1978b "An Anthropological Apologetic for the Homogeneous Unit Principle in Missiology." *Occasional Bulletin of Missionary Research* 10: 121-126.

1978c "Worldview in Intercultural Communication." In *Intercultural and International Communication,* edited by Fred L. Casmir. Lanham, MD: University Press of America.

1978d "Christianity and Culture in Africa." In *Facing the New Challenges—the Message of PACLA*. Pp. 286-91. Nairobi: Evangel Publishing House.

1978e "The Church in Western Africa" (Response #2). In *The Church in Africa 1977*, by Charles R. Taber. Pasadena, CA: William Carey Library.

1978f "Interpreting in Cultural Context." *Journal of the Evangelical Theological Society* 21: 357-67.

1979a "Dynamic Equivalence Churches in Muslim Society." In *The Gospel and Islam: A 1978 Compendium*, edited by Donald M. McCurry. Monrovia, CA: MARC.

1979b "God's Model for Communication." *Ashland Theological Bulletin* (entitled *Communicating the Gospel God's Way*, chapter 1) 12(1, Spring): 3-16.

1979c "The Credibility of the Message and the Messenger." *Ashland Theological Bulletin* (entitled *Communicating the Gospel God's Way*, chapter 2) 12(1, Spring): 17-32.

1979d "What is the Receptor Up To?" *Ashland Theological Bulletin* (entitled *Communicating the Gospel God's Way*, chapter 3) 12(1, Spring): 33-42.

1979e "The Power of Life Involvement." *Ashland Theological Bulletin* (entitled *Communicating the Gospel God's Way*, chapter 4) 12(1, Spring): 43-60.

1979f "Dynamic Equivalence Theologizing." In *Readings in Dynamic Indigeneity*, edited by C. H. Kraft and T. N. Wisley. Pp. 258-85. Pasadena, CA: William Carey Library. Reprinted from *Christianity in Culture*. Maryknoll, NY: Orbis, 1979, pp. 231-311.

1979g "Measuring Indigeneity." In *Readings in Dynamic Indigeneity*, edited by C. H. Kraft and T. N. Wisley. Pp. 118-52. Pasadena, CA: William Carey Library.

1980a "Conservative Christians and Anthropologists: A Clash of Worldviews." *Journal of the American Scientific Affiliation* 32(September): 140-145.

1980b "The Church in Culture—A Dynamic Equivalence Model." In *Down to Earth: Studies in Christianity and Culture*, edited by John R.W. Stott and Robert Coote. Pp. 211-230. Grand Rapids, MI: William B. Eerdmans Publishing Company.

1981 "The Place of the Receptor in Communication." *Theology, News and Notes* 28(3, October): 13-15, 23.

1982a Foreword in *Oral Communication of the Scripture* by Herbert V. Klem. Pasadena, CA: William Carey Library.

1982b "My Distaste for the Combative Approach." *Evangelical Missions Quarterly* 18(3, July): 139-142.

1983 Foreward in *Guidelines for Christian Theology in Africa* by Osadolor Imasogie Achimota. Ghana: Africa Christian Press.

1986a "Worldview and Bible Translation." *Notes on Anthropology* 6 and 7 (June-September): 46-57.

1986b "The Question of Miracles." *The Pentecostal Minister*, Winter, 24-27.

1986c "Supracultural Meanings via Cultural Forms." In *A Guide to Contemporary Hermeneutics*, edited by Donald K. McKim. Pp. 309-343. Grand Rapids, MI: William B. Eerdmans Publishing Company.

1987a "Missionary and SIL/WBT." In *Current Concerns of Anthropologists and Missionaries*, edited by Karl J. Franklin. Pp. 133-142. Dallas, TX: SIL.

1987b "Shifting Worldviews, Shifting Attitudes." In *Riding the Third Wave*, edited by John Wimber and Kevin Springer. Pp. 122-134. England: Marshall Pickering.

1990 "Shifting Worldviews, Sifting Attitudes." In *Conflict and Conquest, Power Encounter Topics for Taiwan*, edited by Kenneth D. Shay. Taiwan: O C International.

1991 "What Kind of Encounters Do We Need in Our Christian Witness?" *Evangelical Missions Quarterly* 27(3, July): 258-265.

1992 "Allegiance, Truth and Power Encounters in Christian Witness." In *Pentecost, Mission and Ecumenism*. Essays on Intercultural Theology, edited Jan. A.B. Jongeneel. New York: Peter Lang.

1993 "Understanding and Valuing Multiethnic Diversity," with Marguerite G. Kraft. *Theology News and Notes* 40(4): 6-8.

1994a "Two Kingdoms in Conflict." In *Behind Enemy Lines*, edited by Charles Kraft. Ann Arbor, MI: Servant Books.

1994b "Spiritual Power: Principles and Observations." In *Behind Enemy Lines*, edited by Charles Kraft. Ann Arbor, MI: Servant Books.

1994c "Dealing with Demonization." In *Behind Enemy Lines*, edited by Charles Kraft. Ann Arbor, MI: Servant Books.

# APPENDIX II - A SYMPHONIC APPROACH TO INTER-DISCIPLINARY INTEGRATION: A VARI-DYNAMIC MODEL[2]

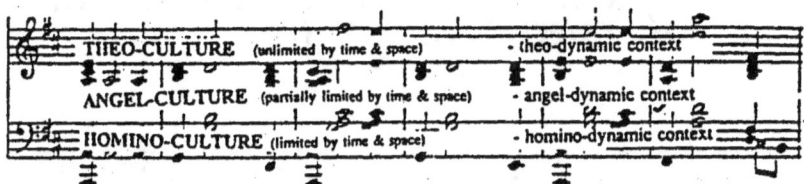

**THEO-CULTURE**     *(theo-dynamic context)*

trinitario-dynamics:    Trinity, Christology, pneumatology, covenant, etc.
Inspirio-dynamics:    inspiration, illumination, etc.
Soterio-dynamics:    predestination, atonement, etc.

**ANGEL-CULTURE**     *(angel-dynamic context)*

theophano-dynamics:    theophany, vision, dream, etc.
Angelo-dynamics:    angiology, deliverance, etc.
Satano-dynamics:    demonology, power encounter, etc.

**HOMINO-CULTURE**     *(homino-dynamic context)*
Christo-dynamics:    incarnation, missianology, etc.
Missio-dynamics:    *missio dei, possessio, elenctic,* etc.
Culturo-dynamics:    enculturation, assimilation, westernization, etc.
Socio-dynamics:    socialization, system theory. structural analysis, etc.
Psycho-dynamics:    cognitive analysis, worldview studies, etic/emic, etc.

---

[2]*The "vari-dynamic model" (as in aero-dynamic or thermodynamic model) includes the various dynamic systems within the model.*

160 MISSIOLOGY AND THE SOCIAL SCIENCES

Behavioral-dynamics: reciprocity, kinesics, proxemics, etc.
Linguistic-dynamics: descriptive linguistics, semantics, etc.

# APPENDIX III - A SYNOPSIS OF REVELATION, INSPIRATION AND ILLUMINATION
(Wan 1994:6)

|  | Revelation | Inspiration | Illumination |
|---|---|---|---|
| Key Question | What is communicated? | How is it communicated? | Why is it communicated? |
| Answer | the material / message communicated | the method of recording | the meaning of record |
| Focus- What | the product | the process | the practical and spiritual enlightenment |
| - Who | the revealer, the author | the instrumental Bible writers | the receiver of the message |
| Objective | the communication of God's message to man | the complete infallibility of God's message through man | man through the Holy Spirit (1Co 2:13,14) |
| Objective / Subjective | objective disclosure | objective disclosure and/or subjective appreciation (1Co 7:10, 12, 25, 40) | subjective apprehension |
| Subject | the self-revealing God | God's chosen few | all God's children |
| Time | past historical fact: special revelation e.g. incarnation and inspiration present continued effects: creation and conscience | past historically terminated event: inspiring Bible writers by the Divine Author (Rev 22:18,19) | present process of conviction and conversion |
| Technical Term(s) | Special revelation: i.e. redemptive revelation both in Christ the living Word (incarnation Heb 1:2; Jn 1:14) and | Inscripturation: the process of the inspired truth as infallible and authoritative truth of faith and practice | none |

|  |  |  |  |
|---|---|---|---|
| based on the historic truth | the inspired/inscripturated Word General revelation: creation and conscience (Ps 19; Ro 1 and 2) | Inerrancy: the trustworthiness and truthfulness of God's inspiration Plenary inspiration: all parts of the O.T and N.T. are inspired and infallible | |
| Catchy Phrase | inspiration without revelation as in the Book of Acts (Ac 1:4) | inspiration including revelation as in the Apocalypse (Rev 1:1-11) | inspiration with illumination as in the Prophets (1Pe 1:11) inspiration including illumination as in the case of Paul (1Co 2:12) |
| Similarity | All dealing with God's interaction with humans in terms of the Scripture leading to a better knowledge of God and his plan of salvation for humanity | | |

# APPENDIX IV
## CONTEXTUAL INTERACTION OF THE TRIUNE GOD'S REVELATION TO MAN
(Wan 1994:8) (multi-dimension, multi-level, multi-context)

| CONTEXT\LEVEL | | THE WORK | | | THE WORD | | | THROUGH THE WORD | |
|---|---|---|---|---|---|---|---|---|---|
| theo-culture | | GENERAL REVELATION | H.S. | Son | SPECIAL REVELATION | F.A. | H.S. | INTERPRETATION /TRANSLATION | F.A. Son |
| homino-culture | universe and mankind | | F.A. | | Jesus = God -man Being | Son | | H.S. contemporary interpreter/translator | |
| | CREATION and CONSCIENCE | | | | INCARNATION | | | Bible = divine -human Book | |
| | | | | | | | | INSPIRATION and INSCRIPTURATION | REGENERATION and ILLUMINATION |

# APPENDIX V - GOD'S REVELATION TO MAN (Wan 1994:7)
## (multi-dimension, multi-level, multi-context)

| DIMENSION / CATEGORY | | THE WORD (INCARNATION) | IN THE WORD (INSCRIPTURATION) | THROUGH THE WORD (INTERPRETATION) |
|---|---|---|---|---|
| NATURE OF TRUTH | | essential and efficient | essential: being God's Word | efficient: becoming God's Word |
| PRESENTATION OF TRUTH | | personal and propositional | propositional | personal |
| PERSPECTIVE - CHRISTIAN | | objective and subjective | objective | subjective |
| TIME | | historical and historic | historical | historic |
| PROCESS | | completed and continuous | completed | continuous |
| WORK / LEVEL | divine | the Christ: perfect God | H.S.: Author, inspiring | H.S.: illuminating |
| | human | the Jesus: perfect Man | Bible writers: inspired | interpreter: exegeting |
| PRODUCT | | divine-human Perfect Being | divine-human perfect Book | imperfect efforts need divine aids |
| CON-TEXT | historico- | past and present | past | past -> present |
| | culturo- | dual level: theo-culture homino-culture | multi-faceted: Jewish/Hellenistic /Aramaic/Roman | multiple in no. and variety of cultures |
| | linguistic- | heavenly/Gk./Aramaic/ Hebrews | multi-lingual: Heb./Gk./Aramaic | many contemporary languages |

## APPENDIX VI - THE TWO QUESTIONS: BIBLICAL? SCRIPTURAL?

(Wan 1994:12)

```
            ---->  ==  ---->
biblically based      scripturally sound
            <----  ==  <----
```

-descriptive         -prescriptive
-precedent           -principle
-cultural/           -transcultural/
 temporal             eternal

# 9

# USE AND MISUSE OF THE SOCIAL SCIENCES: INTERPRETING THE BIBLICAL TEXT

### Robertson McQuilkin[1]

As the new executive director of the Evangelical Missiological Society, it might be helpful in getting acquainted to describe my pilgrimage in regard to our theme for the year, "Evangelical Missiology and the Social Sciences." After the personal pilgrimage, let me suggest some principles for doing our missiology under the authority of Scripture. Only as we carefully identify the meaning intended by the Bible authors will we be able to use the social sciences with profit and avoid having our missiology skewed by some naturalistically-based theory.

## INTRODUCTION: MY PERSONAL PILGRIMAGE

When getting my education in the forties, anthropology was not part of the missionary's preparation, so I got special permission from the seminary dean, Harold Lindsell, to take some of my electives at the nearby University of California at Los Angeles. The only courses available were marginal to my purpose, though they did introduce me to the discipline which I sensed could be helpful to an aspiring missionary. In the fifties I subscribed to *Practical Anthropology* and bought everything published by Eugene Nida. This was getting closer to what I had in mind, but I still lacked the foundations, so in the late fifties I ordered basic anthropological textbooks and conducted my self-

---

[1] Robertson McQuilkin is president emeritus of Columbia International University.

education on-site in Japan. But these sources were not helping with what Donald McGavran was later to call "church growth anthropology," which is what I was interested in as a church planter, though I didn't know the terminology. Years later McGavran advised me, when I returned to the presidency of Columbia International University (then Columbia Bible College), "You must find and employ *church growth* anthropologists. Not traditional historic anthropologists and not just cultural anthropologists," he said, "not just applied cultural anthropologists and not just applied cultural missionary anthropologists. You must get church growth anthropologists!"

Before McGavran burst on the missions scene, however, I was sensing that anthropology must be focused on getting the task done, so I began the serious study of the Japanese value system. I wanted to know what Japanese valued, not what I valued. For pre-evangelism I wanted to connect with some motivational point for which our faith offered help. I was astounded to discover that many things important to me were of little or no importance to Japanese: eternal life, propositional truth, individual freedom, forgiveness of sin, a personal God, history. These were things I had been trying to market. At the same time I found things important to the Japanese that were not priorities for most westerners, but, I discovered, things to which Scripture speaks: approval and sense of belonging, security, relationships, feelings, honor of parents, present "salvation," obligation, loyalty, beauty, love of nature, and the value of suffering. My work was thoroughly researched and of great significance for any evangelistic approach, but evangelical missionaries were not interested. So I published in the ecumenical journal *Japan Christian Quarterly*.[2]

These studies prepared me for the dawn of McGavran and the church growth movement in the sixties. Great controversy raged as many evangelicals opposed the movement. This drove me to examine Scripture. Well, actually, to examine McGavran. Since he was a quintessential pragmatist he did not favor us with a statement of his presuppositions, let alone an analysis of any biblical basis for them. So first I had to analyze what he was saying and distill the presuppositions, and then examine them in the light of Scripture. Though he did not engage

---

[2]*The Japan Christian Quarterly*, Fall, 1967.

in such activity, he agreed that my analysis was accurate, proving his agreement by asking me to report my findings as a lectureship in his school. I found that most of McGavran's basic ideas, including his use of anthropology, were either demanded by Scriptural teaching or permitted by it.³ I was trying to bring the insights of anthropology under the functional authority of Scripture. Anthropology was a legitimate tool of missiology, if pursued rigorously under the authority of God-revealed truth about human nature and relationships. But many evangelical missionaries at the time did not agree that it was legitimate at all, and few used the tool.

Imagine my surprise, then, in the early seventies, when Donald McGavran said to me, "Robertson, the major battle in missions during the rest of this century will be with anthropology." As was often the case, the old gentleman was uncanny in sensing the future before it arrived. But he put me onto something important. Though anthropological insights were rapidly gaining acceptance in the world of missions, not all of them were examined in the light of Scripture. The end result was a flood of unbiblical and even anti-biblical ideas and practice. Not all of this is attributable to anthropology, of course, since our whole society has moved into a relativistic, postmodern approach to life. But the social sciences, either as the firstborn of postmodern thinking or as a parent of it, bypassed what Scripture had to say about human nature and society. So it was that, beginning in the seventies, I wrote on themes relating to doing social science under the authority of Scripture.⁴ I who had so vigorously advocated the use of these tools was not defending against their misuse.

Sensing that the basic problem was hermeneutics, I began to address it in that context, especially in the eighties. Traditionally, hermeneutics had dealt with correct exegesis, getting at the meaning intended by the author.⁵ Very little atten-

---

³*Measuring the Church Movement*, Chicago: Moody (1973, 74).

⁴"The Behavioral Sciences Under the Authority of Scripture," *Journal of the Evangelical Theological Society*, March 1977; "Limits of Cultural Interpretation," *JETS*, June 1980; "Problems of Normativeness in Scripture: Cultural Versus Permanent," in *Hermeneutics, Inerrancy, and the Bible*, pp. 219-240, Grand Rapids: Zondervan Publishing Co., 1984.

⁵Note that I use the term "hermeneutics" in its normal meaning, "the science of interpretation," not as it is used by Paul Hiebert (*Anthropological*

tion had been given to principles for making valid application, determining what God intended as a response to his revelation. The bypass of scriptural authority by evangelical scholars was not taking place so much in the interpretation of the meaning, but in the application of that meaning, identifying the significance of the teaching for us today. Thus, I sought to develop a "hermeneutics" of application so that we could use our cultural tools authentically.

Though my hermeneutics text has been widely used and quoted, I was too late. Under the impact of postmodern thinking, many of our evangelical theologians have moved into the camp of partial relativism, or, as some have called it,"relative relativism." In this way theological colleagues, using cultural tools for understanding and applying Scripture, have exposed the flank of our missiology forces by stripping away the defense of a Scripture held to be normative for contemporary obedience. In response to this, I and colleague Brad Mullen presented a paper at the Evangelical Theological Association annual meeting in November 1994, "The Impact of Postmodern Thinking on Evangelical Hermeneutics," in which we argued that an understanding of the culture of the author of Scripture and of the recipient is helpful in identifying the meaning intended by the author and the response intended by the Holy Spirit, but if such understanding is used to alter the meaning or set aside the authority for contemporary obedience, we have forfeited the authority of Scripture. So I began to sense that in a postmodern age, it has become increasingly hazardous to use the tools of Western social science to build our missiology.

This, in brief, has been my pilgrimage. So I come to you today to plead the cause of scriptural authority in all our mis-

---

*Insights for Missionaries*, Grand Rapids:Baker, 1985, p. 19) who apparently follows the lead of Nida (Eugene A. Nida and William D. Reyburn, *Meaning Across Cultures: A Study on Biblical Translating*, New York: Orbis, 1981) who gives a new definition:"Hermeneutics...may be described as pointing out parallels between the biblical message and present-day events and determining the extent of relevance and the appropriate response for the believer," p. 30. Ascribing the task of applying the meaning of Scripture to the current context (often called "the significance of the text") to the interpretative role is not a matter of mere semantics. It paves the way for allowing the current context to determine, not merely the significance, but increasingly, the meaning of the text.

siological endeavors, especially when we use the tools provided by the social sciences. First, then, let us outline a few of the benefits of using the tools of anthropology appropriately under the authority of Scripture, and then some of the perils when this is not done.

## BENEFITS OF ANTHROPOLOGY FOR MISSIONS

### To Sensitize to Cultural Factors for More Effective Communication

The study of cross-cultural communication in the preparation of missionaries has become an accepted norm so that comment or illustration is hardly necessary. Nevertheless, ethnocentric thinking and behavior is so ingrained and so unconscious that the missionary needs the constant prodding of cultural sensitizers. The husband who hangs out diapers to dry may be commendable in American society, but if he does so in some societies it may irreparably damage the reputation of his wife. He may carefully guard himself from questionable behavior toward the opposite sex only to discover that a far greater offence is impatience. Cultural anthropology can be a missionary's best friend in opening his eyes to biblical norms he had never considered, so that he can communicate cross-culturally more effectively. And, at the same time, prove to be more biblically authentic.

### To Identify Values for Pre-evangelism

The young Japanese man was soundly converted and grew like an amaryllis. About six months after his conversion he came to me. "Sensei, you always talk about heaven and I've said to myself, 'Who wants that? One life is enough!' But now that I've gotten acquainted with Jesus I really want to go there to be with him forever." I had been trying to entice with visions of heaven a people whose idea of paradise is cessation of existence, to get off the wheel of reincarnation altogether. I was using bad bait. Cultural anthropology is a great tool to discover the values and non-values of a people so that the missionary can start with good news about what is valued—and biblical—not with what is valueless to the hearer.

**To Strengthen Evangelism of the Sincere Seeker**

The twenty-five-year veteran missionary looked despondent when she should have been exuberant a week before her fifth furlough. I asked what was so distressing and she told a sad story. The centerpiece of this term's ministry had been a highly successful Bible study with a group of physicians. The night before, at her farewell party, the leader of the group had told her, "Now I understand what you are teaching about Christianity and I want you to know I believe it." Elated, she responded, "Wonderful! You've become a Christian!" The physician was startled and blurted out, "A Christian? Oh, no! I said I believed it was true, but that doesn't have anything to do with me personally." My heart went out to the dejected veteran but I wondered, "Why hasn't anyone told her that Japanese aren't interested in propositional truth when it comes to religion?" A very intelligent, left-brained logician, she had been selling—for twenty-five years—something very important to her in which they simply were not interested. They wanted to know, "What will this religion do for me—*today*?" Certainly the gospel offers much for today, but that is not necessarily what is uppermost in the missionary's mind.

I called out to the Christian bookstore manager in the next room, "There is a book on this desk. Do you believe that?" "Yes, of course, Sensei, if you say so," he responded. "Well, it's there because you believe it is, but if you didn't believe that, it wouldn't be there." I was preparing a sermon for Christians on evidences for the existence of God and wrestling with the issue that to so many eastern peoples God exists for those who believe in him, but not for those who don't. Though I did not try to change unbelievers into my image in order to preach the gospel, I did feel it important to deliver believers from the ancient East's version of contemporary western postmodern thinking in which reality is concocted of my perceptions. Hirota opened the door and said, "Huh? What did you say?" "I said, if you believe this books is here, it is, but if you don't, it isn't." He exclaimed with astonishment, "Chimpunkampun!" which, by interpretation, is "fool stupidity!" So I changed the sentence slightly, "If you believe God is there he is, but if you don't he's not." "Oh," replied Hirota, "now I understand."

Cultural studies can help the missionary communicate the gospel to people whose view of reality is radically different from his own. I stopped using western apologetics in my effort to convince unbelievers, while seeking to lead believers away from unbiblical views of reality.

Do I spend time seeking to bring the serious seeker under conviction of sin (which, in a shame culture, he may not even recognize as existing) by stressing what he is so constantly guilty of—lying? It's a big one for me. Why can't he see it? Because, as his proverb instructs him, "A lie also is a useful thing." My attempts to convict him of the heinousness of such a sin will no doubt prove futile, but if I switch to sins he is acutely aware of, like relationships he has broken or failure to meet his eternal obligations to his parents, I might make some progress in bringing conviction of sin. And both my theology and good psychology teach me a person must have that before he is eligible for salvation. I might even switch to shame instead of sin as an entering wedge, if shame is what his tightly knit culture recognized. After all, it is a shameful thing to fail in our obligations to God and forgiveness of that shameful offence might prove desirable.

William Pencille was trying to reach the Ayore tribe in Bolivia.

> There were a few dried-up oranges on a tree in my yard and I wanted them for my children, so I warned the Indians not to touch them. But some boys took them and I gave them a good tongue-lashing. The Indians were shocked: this man, preaching against adultery and murder, was selfish and angry! Who could understand his strange ways and his God?[6]

Cultural anthropology can alert the foreigner to the blocks to effective evangelism created by his own cultural entrapment, not to mention his unbiblical attitudes and behavior. But it can also positively assist in developing more effective

---

[6]"Bridging the Gap From Stone Age to Space Age," *Evangelical Missions Quarterly*, Fall, 1967, p. 23.

communication. Don Richardson speaks of redemptive analogies he believes exist in all cultures, using his experience of the Peach Child as an example.[7] Subsequently he studies thirty-five other cultures and says that every one has a cultural pass-key. Though I never discovered a local belief that so graphically illustrated the sacrifice of God's Son as the peace child, I did discover many values that Scripture advocates. This is no doubt the result of general revelation, the imprint of God's image that even centuries of error cannot fully efface. For example, God loves beauty and so do the Japanese. American missionaries often do not. While the temples and their ground are places of exquisite beauty, we erect quonset huts with no garden at all and call them churches.

Another example. We value individualism, rugged individualism. Otherwise we would never havebecome missionaries. The problem is, we try to convert people into our image in order for them to qualify for receiving our message. The person who won't stand out against family and friends is not worthy. Yet, the African or Asian may not think such a trait desirable at all. He may value contrasting virtues which we give slight attention, even though they may be major biblical themes. Community and loyalty, for example, honor of parents and human relationships, acceptance and affirmation are biblical attitudes which don't mix easily with individualism. Individual responsibility is a major strand of biblical teaching but it is not the only strand and can become demonic when not held in tension with balancing characteristics. Our own western civilization may yet prove that. In a society in which a person's all-important security is provided by those who guarantee his life, his family and employer, the offer of freedom and independence may not sound like good news. We must include in our message values which we may have overlooked in our ethnocentric astigmatism if we are to be true to the whole revelation of God's will for us humans and if we are to convince people that we bring truly good news. Thus, church growth anthropology—anthropological insights for more effective evangelism—will assist.

---

[7] Don Richardson, *Peace Child*, Regal, 1974.

## To Assist in Formulating an Indigenous Theology and Pastoral Approaches

My conviction is that only a spiritually mature indigenous church can make a full integration of biblical truth with the local culture, true to that culture and true to Scripture. The foreigner should always be modest about his insights. Of course, the indigenous church leadership may have been so acculturated to western concepts that they, too, could benefit from the insights of anthropology, but the missionary's basic stance should be one of learning.

For example, what is the objective of counseling? To enable a person to break free and assert his or her own rights with vigor and without a sense of guilt? I shall never forget the eerie feeling, in reading the first popular Japanese treatment of psychiatry, to discover the commonality with Western approaches to treatment until it came to the goal. There, for a person to be well, meant conformity. Until the counselor could help him relate to others in that way, his patient was destroying himself with antisocial behavior. The goal was the opposite of Western therapy. Or take marriage counseling. The chief obstacles to unity in marriage, it is said, are money, sex, and one's approach to child rearing. What could be more culturally specific? And yet we spend lavishly to get our books about marriage translated into other languages without getting them translated into other cultures.

Consider suffering. In the triumphal aftermath of World War II and the euphoria of an expanding economy, what missionary would have written on the pain of God? Who among us worked at integrating this characteristic into his message, let alone into his life? Yet this is precisely what Japanese theologianl Kazoh Kitamori did in his volume *Theology of the Pain of God*.[8]

Stealing—taking by force what is not rightfully mine—is wrong by biblical standards in any culture, but culture defines "what is rightfully mine." Native Americans no doubt wished the Western invaders had studied anthropology. Maybe they wouldn't have staked out claims to private ownership of what had been public land!

---

[8]Richmond: John Knox, 1958.

My first term, before completing an anthropological analysis of Japanese values, I trained the new believers in various leadership roles. We did TEE before it was invented and many became effective leaders. On the American model. I was confident it was the New Testament model. But the first national pastor of that thriving church took as his primary responsibility squeezing out of the fellowship all "my" leaders. They didn't fit the cultural pattern; they were an intolerable threat to him. The second term, following my anthropological studies, we had similar evangelistic success, but I trained leadership on the Japanese model of leadership and the pastor who followed lost none of them.

This does not mean that the foreigner must abandon scriptural principles, of course. For example, we were applying for accreditation and as president of the Christian college, I was responsible for the final application papers for the government. I had frequent conflicts with the senior faculty member in charge of the preparation. I could not let falsehoods go in the report. After some months of unsuccessfully seeking to change my view of "true" and "false," the professor said, "Well, Sensei, it just may be that a lie is the cross God will ask you to bear." We decided against taking up that "cross" because I could not abdicate my conscience. But most of the strong ethical, pastoral, and doctrinal stands I was tempted to take against my Japanese brothers were ill-advised. I had to learn to sit under their tutelage.

Another important area for integration is the creation of functional substitutes for unacceptable rites and festivals. Is New Year's the chief celebration period of the year? The missionary must not merely forbid participation in a religion-intensive festival and expect seekers and new believers simply to abstain and sit at home while all the family and, indeed, the whole nation celebrates. Is there a solemn rite of passage into adulthood in the African tribe, a rite filled with anti-biblical behavior and attitudes? What substitute rite, of equal significance and excitement, can the missionary or church introduce? I cringe to think of the ordeal through which those early Christians in my ministry had to pass. Baptism scrunched up in a home *ofuro* (a small wooden tub), a public bathhouse, a muddy, shallow river in the open countryside with no place to change clothes. Cultural insensitivity had added unnecessary barriers.

Even the agenda the preacher addresses needs to be related to felt needs, though often the prophet must raise to a place of "felt" some biblical but unrecognized needs. My contention is that the person within the culture is best equipped for both of these endeavors. When I lived for a time in inner city Atlanta I visited sixteen black churches. Though they ranged from the lowest to highest economic levels, in every case the agenda was social justice and the hope of heaven. In the midst of this immersion experience I attended a white Christian business executives' breakfast and could hardly escape the fact that the theme of message, testimonies and prayer requests were all economically oriented and thoroughly tied to this earth, not heaven. And not a word about social justice! That weekend I found myself in an adult Sunday school class in a large church in Bradenton, Florida, a retirement capitol of the nation. Everything in the lesson and in the many prayer requests had to do with ill health and the deceased. If I, a healthy fifty-year old Christian worker, white and middle class, had been asked to speak to any of these groups I would never have addressed any of those topics. And might not have connected with the audience at all. People on the inside are best able to identify biblically legitimate felt needs.

Generations of missionaries in Africa insisted that polygamists must divorce all wives but one in order to qualify for church membership. In other words, they forced the men to commit a sin roundly condemned by Scripture (divorce) in order to correct a practice which was more heinous in their view (polygamy), even if it was not directly condemned in Scripture. Had they studied Scripture through the lens of their adoptive culture, they might have come to different conclusions and saved untold misery for the divorced wives who had no place to go.

The social sciences help the missionary ask the questions that have not been asked and find solutions that are at once biblically authentic and culturally attuned. But the tools can be hazardous.

## HAZARDS IN USING THE TOOLS OF ANTHROPOLOGY

The former executive director of the Evangelical Missiological Society, David Hesselgrave, wrote in 1994,

"Missiology itself has become more and more dependent upon the social sciences while its foundation in biblical revelation shows signs of gradual erosion . . . Edward Rommen fears that missiology is being 'detheologized.'"[9] I'm not convinced this trend is so recent. In the July 1979 issue of *MARC*, Ed Dayton traced the history of the emerging "new science of missiology" and described it as a combination of research, communications (derived, he said, from anthropology, sociology, and psychology) and management theory. The result of this "new science" so derived was reflected in a note I received from a graduate student in 1984 who was agonizing over his gradual loss of missionary passion as he studied anthropology and cross-cultural communication in one of our premier evangelical seminaries. He said the more he studied he realized two things: because of the cultural encapsulation of Scripture and his own entrapment in ethnocentrism he was not sure of the truth of any message he might give. Secondly, he was quite convinced that even if he could salvage some "truth," he could never communicate it cross-culturally, so high and complex were the barriers. Ron was no minimal-exposure college student. This graduate student appended a list of eighteen leading evangelical anthropologists and theologians whose books and articles he had read. I encountered a similar experience in many graduate students from many schools throughout the seventies and eighties. Many hot-hearted young men and women lost the vision of missionary service.

Indeed there are hazards. And what are they? Often culture is used as a grid for determining what in Scripture is normative rather than using Scripture as the grid to determine what in culture is acceptable. How do we go about bringing proposed concepts or methods under the authority of Scripture?

First, using all the principles for valid interpretation we search out the meaning intended by the author of every pertinent text. For example, in my own text twelve such "guidelines for

---

[9]*Scripture and Strategy: The Use of the Bible in Postmodern Church and Mission*, David Hesselgrave, Pasadena: William Carey Library, 1994. Hesselgrave refers in this quotation to his *Today's Choices for Tomorrow's Mission: An Evangelical Perspective On Trends and Issues in Missions*, Grand Rapids, MI: Zondervan Publishing House, 1988, and Rommen's, "The Detheologization of Missiology," in *The Trinity World Forum*, Winter, 1994.

interpretation" are elucidated, and the neglect of any one of them will jeopardize the outcome. But simply correctly identifying the meaning of the text does not assure that it will function as the authority in the life of the missionary or the church. Valid guidelines must be followed to determine the audience God intended and the response he desires from us if the teaching is indeed intended for us. We must ask key questions of the concept or activity: What is the basic idea? Is this explicitly declared to be the will of God? If "yes," is it in balance with other teaching? If it is not explicitly declared to be the will of God, is it demanded by clear biblical principle? If not, is it compatible with explicit teaching and clear principle? Putting these questions in a flow chart (see page 178) may assist in bringing anthropological concepts under the functional authority of Scripture.[10]

Consider some examples of contemporary missiology gone astray.

### Theological Issues: Hell and the Way of Salvation

Increasing numbers of Bible scholars and missiologists who consider themselves evangelical are calling into question the traditional ideas about hell and the way of salvation. The first question to ask, a question often skipped, is, "What are we talking about?" In other words, definition must come first. Are you advocating universalism, that all will ultimately be saved? Or are you advocating that many may be saved without the knowledge of Christ? After determining what the issue actually is, that concept must be rigorously examined in the light of Scripture. Have we identified all passages which deal with the issue and have we examined all other teachings of Scripture which correlate with this teaching? Having identified all the passages, not a select few, have we done the rigorous work of applying all principles of interpretation to determine the meaning intended by the author of each passage and correlating all those passages and all those doctrines? For example, have we given decisive weight to the clear teaching over the obscure text, to the abundant teaching over the occasional, to the New Testament over the Old? Only with such rigorous, honest work can we

---

[10]*Understanding and Applying the Bible*, p. 312.

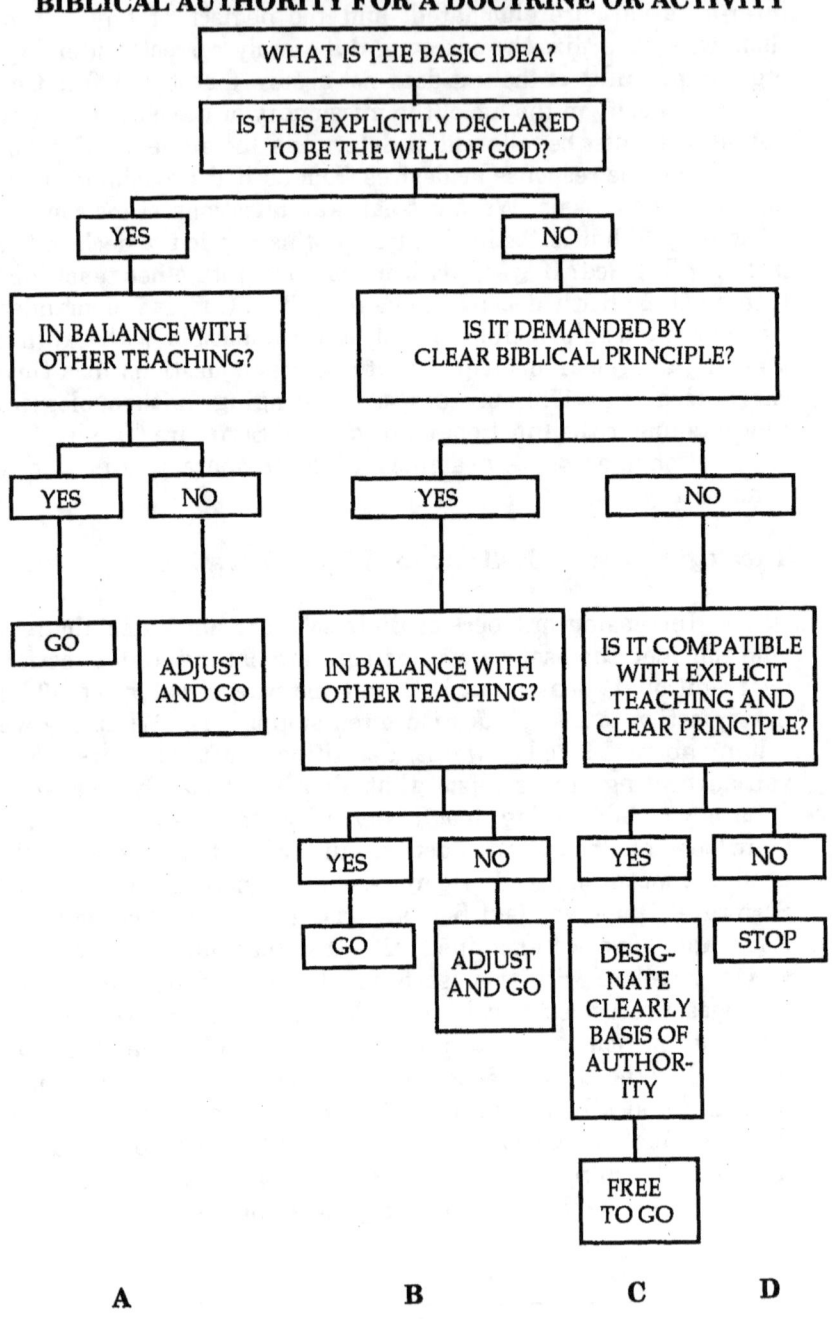

claim to be doing missions under the functional authority of Scripture.

Increasingly, the way of salvation is being redefined and the lostness of those out of Christ is being called into question. For example, when salvation is treated as a direction, not an event, so that Muslims are acceptable to God when headed in the right direction, godward, culture has imposed its authority over Scripture in the most critical of missionary affirmations.[11] Again, increasing numbers of those who consider themselves evangelical no longer believe in hell—it doesn't fit the postmodern mentality.[12] And that is in process of cutting the nerve of the missionary enterprise. Scripture is not in functional control of missiological reasoning when such conclusions emerge.

**Ethical Issues**

According to some interpreters, Christ's teaching against divorce, Paul's teaching against homosexuality, and biblical norms for the role of the woman in marriage are all culturally bound teachings and not normative. Therefore, they do not demand obedience in every culture of every age. I was once seated across the luncheon table from an anthropologist who was head of linguistics in a major mission. We were discussing the question of what teachings in Scripture are normative.

> "What do you think," I asked, "should be required of all people in every tribe and culture?"
>
> He responded immediately, "Those teachings which are culturally universal."
>
> "For example?"
>
> "Well . . . " He hesitated. "I'm not altogether sure."
>
> "Something like forbidding murder?" I suggested.

---

[11]See, for example, Charles Kraft, *Christianity in Culture*, Maryknoll: Orbis, 1979, pp. 231, 240, 241, 250.

[12]James Davison Hunter, *Evangelicalism: The Coming Generation*, Chicago: University of Chicago Press, 1987, pp. 33, 34. Note that Hunter lays the lion's share of the blame for loss of evangelical convictions our evangelical colleges on the faculty in the sciences and humanities, p. 175.

"Why, yes," he said, "that would be a cultural universal."

"I am surprised to hear that," I replied. "I would have thought that killing and perhaps even eating the victim, would be a virtue in some societies."

"Well, I guess you're right."

This is doing Scripture under the authority of anthropological principles, not doing anthropology under the authority of Scripture.

Or take liberation theology. Let us run it through the flow chart. The first question we must ask is, "Precisely what do you mean by 'liberation theology'?" Do you mean that we should preach a holistic good news, that Christ liberates both from the results of sinful behavior and from the behavior itself so that the true Christian will seek justice and mercy in society? Or do you mean that we must bring about justice and mercy by taking up arms to enforce it? Is violence in the cause of the gospel demanded by Scripture in direct teaching or in principle? Since it obviously is not, the next question must be asked, is it compatible with scriptural teaching? Since Christ taught expressly against such a concept (Mt 26:52), the Christian is conscience-bound to reject it. Actually, classical "liberation theology" was based deliberately on "culture" and "history" as the authority, with Scripture as a sometime resource for selected examples of God at work in history.

To run certain issues through the flow chart, such as oppression, injustice, poverty, is quickly to establish a biblical authority for addressing the issue for others, such as racism and sexism, is to find biblical principles on which to build. But if the agenda or the approach toward biblically valid issues is built from extra-biblical sources, one may quickly lose biblical authority.

**Power Encounter**

In a remote jungle base in Latin America the translators were giving reports at the annual meeting. One translator reported how she had finally resolved the problem of translating "demon" for a people who didn't recognize their existence. She had translated demonic references as "illness." This is doing theology by translation under the authority of culture.

Some may go the opposite direction, also guided by culture more than by Scripture. In the EMS second volume for 1995, *Spiritual Power and Missions: Raising the Issues*, we seek to examine the claims and counterclaims on this issue, but primarily we are concerned to probe the biblical foundations of each position. Robert Priest and his associates hold that some of the contemporary power encounter themes are not biblically based, Chuck Kraft responds, and then Patrick Johnstone emphasizes the biblical theme of prayer. Not all are happy with the outcome, but we have attempted to provide a volume that does what I advocate here: wrestle with the issues within the ring of biblical data authentically interpreted and applied. That is the arena in which we must do our missiology and hold one another accountable.

**"Reaching" the "Nations"**

I recently discovered a ten-year-old sermon promoting missions in which I had originally written that there are 12,000 unreached people groups in the world. The number has been crossed out and "6,000" inked in. I smiled. If I used that sermon now, I'd have to cross out that number and put in the contemporary verity, 2,000. Why the confusion? Part of the reason is that we can't agree on what a "people group" is—an ethno-linguistic group or a "group in which the gospel can move without encountering cultural or linguistic barriers." The confusion is compounded by our inability to reach agreement on what "reached" and "unreached" mean. Not to mention uncertainty about what "evangelized" and "unevangelized" mean. Or "Christian" for that matter. The list goes on.

We might dissipate some of the confusion if we stuck with biblical definitions of the task of the church and clearly identified as extra-biblical but pragmatically defensible other definitions, goals, and programs. For the sake of pointing toward a solution, let me suggest a simple statement of biblical definitions as I see them: the initial or evangelistic task of the church is to see that every person on earth hears the gospel with understanding and that a congregation of regenerated people is established in every community; the ongoing task of the church is to disciple the believers for impact on the community at large.

I suggest that in order to achieve the evangelistic task it is quite legitimate to divide up the peoples of the world into segments smaller than contemporary nation-states, using the tools of anthropology and sociology to do so. It is also legitimate to divide up the final goal into do-able segments, such as establishing "an evangelizing church movement" in each people group (however defined) or starting a congregation in each group, or setting a percentage target such as five percent of the total population claiming to be Christians. This could help in strategizing and mobilization. But if the aura of scriptural authority is cast over such definitions and strategies by implying that by reaching a limited objective we have fulfilled the mandate of Jesus Christ, we are not doing our mission under the authority of Scripture and will ultimately inhibit, not advance, the cause of world evangelization. Also, we will confuse God's people. Not to mention, missiologists!

If definitions and strategies derived from extra-biblical sources are held and promoted as pragmatic approaches rather than as biblical mandates, we will free people and organizations to pursue them on that basis. For example, such an approach would free some to concentrate on the "Bibleless" tribes. Others might concentrate on the initial penetration of all homogeneous groups that have no witnessing church movement. Again, others might devote their resources to the full evangelization of large groups that are still out of reach of effective gospel witness. In other words, since Scripture does not describe what the evangelistic task will look like when it is finished, we can get on with the task of being sure that every person on earth has the opportunity to hear the gospel, and that a congregation of God's people is established in every community. And until that goal is accomplished, the church cannot say, "It is finished. The task you gave us to do we have accomplished." God may choose to say "It is finished" before we do, but obedience to the command means that the church must pursue the goal of evangelization and church planting until then. To have more restricted, targeted goals is legitimate for tactical purposes as part of the overall task, but it is not biblical to make a limited goals and market it as the task of the church.

## CONCLUSION

If one ministry approach is considered better than other options because of research data, let us state openly the basis of our recommendation and not paper it over with a few biblical texts and treat it as God's own truth. To follow this procedure of allowing a theory based on research or experience to stand on its own merits would have the added benefit of allowing us to adapt to varying cultures and individual circumstances without fear of violating divine mandate.

When the formulation of mission thinking and the planning of mission strategy are accomplished under the functional control of Scripture, and the study of human attitudes and relationships, the missionary enterprise can be strengthened. But if Scripture does not control both endeavors, if naturalistically-based scientific theory skews or displaces the teaching of Scripture on a given subject, to that extent the missionary enterprise suffers loss. Let us covenant together to use every new tool that holds promise of advancing the Cause, while doing so diligently under the functional authority of Scripture. The social sciences must remain no more than a servant, assisting missiologists as they work hard to understand and apply their final authority for missionary faith and practice, the Word of God.

# 10

# THE SOCIAL SCIENCES AND MISSIONS: APPLYING THE MESSAGE

## Paul G. Hiebert[1]

The history of relationships between missions and anthropology is a long and checkered one. After the Emancipation Act of 1833 that ended slavery in England, the abolitionists turned their attention to the welfare of the native peoples in the colonial dependencies. In 1838 they organized the Aborigines Protection Society in London. Early in its history a split took place between those, mostly missionaries and humanitarians, who wanted to help the "natives" by bringing them the "privileges" of European civilization such as education, medicine and the gospel, and those who wanted to study the people and to protect them from Western incursion. The latter group organized the Ethnological Society of London in 1843 for the study of human biological diversity (Reining 1962). By the 1880s anthropology had gained acceptance in the academic community.

In recent years the relationship between anthropologists, and missionaries has been that of half-siblings—drawing on one another and frequently quarreling. Both work with people abroad. Both struggle with the questions of "Others" and "Otherness" (Hiebert 1995a). Many anthropologists have lived with and gotten much of their field data from missionaries, and missionaries have benefited from anthropological findings. Nevertheless, the relationship has remained a strained one (Salamone 1986).

---

[1] Paul Hiebert is Professor of Mission at Trinity International University.

Let us examine this relationship briefly and look at the ways the social sciences, particularly anthropology, have influenced evangelical mission for good and for bad (table 1).[2]

## THE THEORY OF EVOLUTION (1840 - 1930 A.D.)

The discovery of a new world populated by previously unknown creatures raised profound theological, economic, political and scientific questions. Were these creatures humans, and in need of salvation? Could they be enslaved or ruled? And what accounted for their diversity? The academic community's response was *anthropology*—the science of Others and Otherness. The church's response was *missions*—ministry to these Others.

One grand unifying theory emerged in anthropology to explain the diversity of human beings. Comte proposed a theory of cultural evolution from savagery to barbarism and finally to civilization. Darwin extended this to the theory of biological evolution. The two together formed a secular history designed to explain human diversity.

**Biological Evolution**

The central question from 1840 to 1900 had to do with the great biological diversity among humans. Missionaries, on the basis of Genesis 1, affirmed the biological unity of all human beings, and the need to bring the gospel to them. Anthropologists split over the issue of human origins. In 1863 the Anthropological Society of Britain broke with the Ethnological Society, arguing that Africans and other "natives" were descendent from lower primates. Because of its views the Anthropological Society found it difficult to condemn the brutal slaughter of the aborigi

---

[2]Catholic missiology has had a long history of interaction with anthropology. During the evolutionary period the Vienna School led by Father Schmidt and Father Grabner played a leading role in showing that the majority of simple tribal societies have a high God concept, thereby discrediting the prevailing theory that the high God and monotheism were late in the evolution of religion. Later Louis Luzbetack has played a key role in giving Catholic Missiology a solid anthropological foundation.

nes of Queensland and Tasmania going on at that time (Reining 1962:5). In 1871 the two organizations merged to form the Anthropological Society, which now affirmed the unity of humankind.

A second question now arose—if all humans are one species, how can we explain the racial differences. The answer, according to anthropologists, lay in biological evolution—humans are the same species but some are more evolved than others. This accounted for their differences. It also justified slavery and colonialism. Europeans had the moral responsibility to help backward "natives" become fully human beings.

Most missionaries rejected the theory of biological evolution, but they were not immune to the spirit of the time that upheld the superiority of the white race. Stephen Neill writes:

> Missionaries in the nineteenth century had to some extent yielded to the colonial complex. Only western man was man in the full sense of the word; he was wise and good, and members of other races, in so far as they became westernized, might share in this wisdom and goodness. But western man was the leader, and would remain so for a very long time, perhaps for ever (Neill 1982:259).

Unlike Spanish Catholics who often settled abroad and intermarried with the local people (as in Goa and Latin America), North European missionaries saw their "home" as the country from which they came, often lived lives segregated from the "natives," and discouraged the marriage of their children with the local people. They looked forward to furloughs and retirement "at home." Western mission agencies also resisted sending African-Americans as missionaries abroad. Even now most African-Americans find it hard to gain acceptance by them.

Another example of racism was the preaching by missionaries in Africa as late as the 1950s that the Africans are under the curse of Ham, and therefore are incapable of ruling themselves (Lumeah 1988). We today reject this interpretation of Scripture, but as Nzash Lumeah points out, it is still widespread among the Africans themselves, many of whom believe that Christian institutions will prosper only if a white person is present. As Billy Graham points out, racism is still a deep sin in European and North American churches and missions which we must confront honestly and openly. All peoples have a sense of racial superiority, but we as whites have a particularly bad dose of it.

**Cultural Evolution**

When studies of race failed to define distinct races and the superiority of one over another, anthropologists turned their attention to cultural differences. Here the grand unifying theory was cultural evolution, a secular imitation of the biblical cosmic history. All humans were incorporated into one cosmic story of progress from simple to complex, from savagery to civilization, and from prelogical to logical. The superiority of Western technology and life was self-evident. It enabled the West to conquer and rule the world. It justified the modern Enlightenment view of history.

In this paradigm, the others were not just prelogical primitives, they were our "ancestors"—*human fossils*. Joseph Conrad captures this view in his description of his trip in Africa:

> We penetrated deeper and deeper into the heart of darkness. . . . But suddenly as we struggled around a bend, there would be a glimpse of peaked grass roofs, a burst of yells, a whirl of black limbs, a mass of hands clapping, of feet stamping, of bodies swaying. . . . It was unearthly, and the men were—No, they were not inhuman. . . . They howled and leaped . . . but what thrilled you was just the thought of their humanity—like yours—the thought of your remote kinship (1950:105).

Regarding E. V. Tyler (1832-1917), one of the founders of anthropology, McGrane writes:

> It's as though Tyler saw the whole world as a museum-drama: on stage one, in the Amazon, for instance we can see act one. Simultaneously, on stage two, in New Guinea, we can see act two, etc.

> The people of the world act out the story of *our* history, and the only audience who can understand the play is, of course, "us." We have the benefit of hindsight: we know how the story ends, we *are* how the story ends (1989:95).

Many missionaries rejected the theory of cultural evolution, but the ideas which were a part of its Zeitgeist were absorbed with the air they breathed. Charles Taber notes:

> The superiority of Western civilization as the culmination of human development, the attribution of that superiority to the prolonged dominance of Christianity, the duty of Christians to share civilization and the gospel with the "benighted heathen"—these were the chief intellectual currency of their lives (1991:71).

The key word here is "civilization." During this era the word "culture" was not used in the ways we use it today.

This Enlightenment agenda shaped the modern mission movement in several ways. First, it led to the Westernization of the church. Wilbert Shenk writes:

> The seventeenth-century New England Puritan missionaries largely set the course for modern missions. They defined their task as preaching the gospel so that Native Americans would be converted and receive personal salvation. The model by which they measured their converts was English Puritan civilization . . . . They gathered these new Christians into churches for nurture and discipline and set up programs to transform Christian Indians into English Puritans (1980:35).

Many missionaries accepted the superiority of Western civilization, and saw it their task to civilize and commercialize as well as Christianize the people they served. They built schools and hospitals alongside churches, and saw science as essential a part of the curriculum as the gospel. This equation of the gospel with Western civilization made the gospel unnecessarily foreign in other cultures.

Second, missions exported the Enlightenment split between supernatural and natural realities. Evolutionists argued that prelogical humans created animism to explain their world. This was full of earth-bound spirits, witchcraft and magical powers. As humans evolved, they developed high, philosophical religions, more logical in character, which displaced animism. Finally they developed science as a new kind of knowledge based on reason, which, in time, would replace religious thought. Missionaries rejected the displacement of religion by science, but assumed that Christianity would automatically displace animism with its belief in earthly spirits and powers. For the most part, they did not take seriously the people's beliefs in spirit possession, witchcraft, divination and magic, and simply denied the reality of these. As a result, many of the old beliefs went underground because the missionaries had not dealt with them or provided Christian solutions to the problems these addressed. Today these underground beliefs are resurfacing around the world and creating havoc in young churches.

Third, the supernatural/natural split contributed to the secularization of nature. Many Western Christians turned to religion to deal with eternal matters such as creation, sin and salvation, and to science to explain the events of everyday life. Diseases were attributed to germs, personality disorders to psychological distortions. Missionaries brought the gospel and planted churches. They also established schools and hospitals. Too often these were seen as based on science. Many who studied in mission schools and hospitals rejected the gospel they heard, but adopted science. As a result, as Newbigin (1966) points out, Christian missions have been a great secularizing force in the non-Christian world.

How do we evaluate the effects of the theory of cultural evolution on missions. On the positive side—and there was a positive side—we must remember that the modern mission era witnessed the greatest Christian outreach the world has ever seen. Too often we in the West feel so guilty about the colonial era that we forget that the missionaries, like explorers, traders, colonial government rulers and even anthropologists were people of their times. Moreover, as Lamin Sanneh (1993) points out, the missionaries gave the people dignity and empowered them by translating Scripture into their languages. We must retell the stories of the thousands of young people who felt the call of God and went to the ends of the earth, suffering great hardships and often laying down their lives. Exploration, colonialism and *pax Britanica* did open the doors for missionaries to serve and plant churches in the most remote corners of the earth. God used imperfect people with imperfect understandings in imperfect conditions to carry out his work in remarkable ways.

Another positive side of this era was the affirmation of the unity of humanity. In missionary circles there was no doubt that all humans are created in the image of God, are fallen and lost, and need salvation through faith in Jesus Christ. It was this deep conviction that drove missionaries to sacrifice their whole lives for the salvation of people they did not know. It was this that led them to build schools, hospitals and agricultural training centers, call for justice and moral rectitude, strive to end infanticide, widow burning, intertribal wars, and identify with the poor and oppressed. As Yusufu Turaki points out, their concern to help the people stood in sharp contrast to the colonial rulers who sought mainly to exploit the people and lands they ruled. In our day, we do not have this driving passion or sacrificial commitment that turned the world upside-down.

On the negative side, the theory of cultural evolution gave rise to Western arrogance, ethnocentrism and colonialism. It also led to a separation (even segregation) between missions (made up of Westerners) and churches (made up of "natives"). The result was the domination of young churches by Western missions, and the inability of young churches to mature into full equals. A hundred years after the founding of the Batak Church in Indonesia, Theodor Müller-Krüger wrote:

> So the missionary became the patriarch, who was readily obeyed, and under whose leadership it was confidently believed that all would go well. Is it surprising that this position of the missionary was taken for granted and reflected in the order of the Church as this developed. The patriarchal structure of the Church was accepted as the only means by which its stability and its future could be safeguarded (Neill 1982:257, citing Theodor Müller-Krüger, *Gemacht zu seinem Volk*, 1961. Centenary volume of the Batak Church. P. 33).

A second consequence was that many missionaries saw little good in the people's cultures on which missionaries could build. Consequently, every aspect of traditional cultures had to be destroyed before Christianity could be built up.

A third consequence was that missionaries increasingly saw Christianity the same as other religions, but also as their fulfillment. David Bosch notes:

> It was, however, not until the arrival on the scene of the theory of evolution in the nineteenth century, the rise of liberal theology, and the birth of the new discipline of comparative religion, that the stage was set for an approach according to which religions could be compared and graded in an ascending scale. In the Western world there was no doubt, however, about which religion stood at the pinnacle. In almost every respect every other religion—even if it might be termed a *praeparatio evangelica*—was deficient when compared with Christianity (1991:479).

## SOCIAL ANTHROPOLOGY (1920 - PRESENT)

Two movements displaced cultural evolutionism in the nineteen-twenties, both emerging out of closer encounters with Others in the process of studying them. The first of these was British structural functionalism started in England by A. R. Radcliffe-Brown (1881-1955), and Bronislaw Malinowki (1884-1942). Both (Radcliffe-Brown in particular) were influenced by the newly emerging science of sociology started by Emile Durkheim in France. Both did anthropological fieldwork and learned to know the Others personally as fully human beings.

At first social anthropologists, such as Sir Edward Evan Evans-Pritchard, sought to give detailed objective descriptions and explanations of other cultures, but they did so using the categories and methods of anthropology. These *etic* analyses viewed human cultures as objects to be studied scientifically.

Bronislaw Malinowski went a step further. He argued that to understand Others we must enter their world, and see it in their categories (*emically*) rather than ours. We must be *participants*-as-observers. We must cross the line and identify ourselves primarily with the people rather than the academy. In so doing he made us aware of the tension between being a participant and an observer at the same time—an insider-outsider, a scientist-native, an observer who knows the native language but speaks in English. After Malinowki, in-depth fieldwork became the hallmark of anthropological methodology.

Social anthropologists studied tribes in Africa and the South Pacific Islands in which tribes were living, functioning realities. They saw each society as unique and wholly *sui generis*—a unique, bounded and more or less successful adaptation to a particular environment. Each was made up of parts that "function" to maintain a harmonious, balanced whole. Each was homogeneous and uniform. Each could be explained fully in terms of "social facts." Religions were seen as social constructs needed to maintain the social order. There was nothing "true" about them. Moreover societies were seen as morally neutral. For people in one society to judge those in another was seen as ethnocentrism and imperialism. There were no supra cultural moral or cognitive universals by which cultures could be evaluated.

Social anthropology has had a profound impact on missions in recent years. The major impact of sociology and social anthropology on mission thinking was through the writings of Donald McGavran, Allen Tippett and the Church Growth School. McGavran showed how social dynamics play a major role in the growth and organization of the church. He introduced such concepts as homogeneous groups, people movements, social receptivity/resistance, and social barriers into the mission literature. The results have been a major paradigm shift in modern mission strategizing.

More recent applications of social theory to missions is the people group movement that defines some seventeen thousand people groups and seeks to plant churches in each of them (in part through the Adopt-a-People movement), and the Ten-Forty Window emphasis which focuses on resistant peoples.

How should we evaluate this impact of social theory on missions? On the positive side, it has made us think in terms of social systems. Prior to this, mission thinking was based largely on geographical thinking. Mission agencies went to Africa, India or China. There they divided the country on the basis of comity, and each mission divided its territory into mission fields with one missionary stationed in each. Missionaries were given responsibility to evangelize a certain number of villages, and toured the countryside holding evangelistic services in each of them. But as McGavran pointed out, geographic distances are not the only, or even major barrier to the proclamation of the gospel. Invisible social walls are very real. People may live a few hundred feet from one another, but socially be a hundred miles apart. We need to understand social structures and social dynamics to understand how churches grow.

A second contribution of church growth thinking was to focus the mission task on planting churches as socially viable institutions that could sustain and proclaim the faith. In this it is an heir of the legacy of H. Venn, R. Anderson and Roland Allen with their stress on indigenous churches. Missions too often had focused on evangelism. Today the goal of many missions is not simply individual conversions, but the planting of living, reproducing churches.

A third contribution was the renewed stress on evangelism and the growth of the church during a time when institutionalization had diverted many missions from their central task. Maintaining churches schools, and hospitals took up most of the efforts of the majority of missions.

On the negative side, the church growth and people groups movements are in danger of social reductionism. Understanding and applying social principles are essential to mission outreach. It is hard, however, for us to integrate these with prayer, for divine guidance, and spiritual living because they are based on a notion of social engineering. If we know the social dynamics, we can bring about success. Moreover, success is measured largely in quantitative terms—in terms of numbers of professed converts. How does this fit with the biblical emphases on faithfulness, hardship, suffering and persecution.

A second limitation is that of the early theories of sociology.[3] The concept of people groups fits tribal societies best, like those social anthropologists used as the basis for their studies. But peasant and urban societies cannot be cut up into distinct, bounded people groups without seriously distorting the picture.

---

[3] Church growth is based largely on social theories of the 1930s - 1950s. It has drawn little from more recent conflict- and dynamic-oriented theories of social systems.

Individuals participate in many different groups and cultural frames (Geertz) and do not fully identify with any one of them. Associations, institutions, and networks are the middle-level organizing principles in urban societies. The major exceptions are recent immigrants who may form distinct ethnic communities. Consequently, we cannot really speak of distinct "people groups" among old time urbanites, nor can we hope to generate people movements to Christ in mature city contexts.

A third weakness is a static view of societies. Healthy ones are organic wholes striving for stasis. There is no place for change or conflict. In mission terms this has led to calls for conversion with a minimum amount of social change, and to an uncritical approach to contextualization. People should be allowed to become Christians with a minimum of social dislocation. All social systems are seen as good if they maintain social order. They cannot be judged as sinful. Consequently, sin is reduced to personal sins, and conversion is to primarily inner personal transformations. But societies are not static, or harmonious. Nor are they inherently good. To argue that they are is to ignore corporate sin and to see the world through the eyes of the dominant parties. All this does not fit well with Paul's call for radical social transformation in the lives of new believers. Moreover, this approach often produces large but theologically shallow churches.[4]

A fourth weakness is a truncated view of culture. British structural functionalism and its offspring including church growth have a strong sense of social organization, and how this plays itself out in the lives of people. This includes such concepts as "homogeneous groups," "people movements," and "receptivity-resistance axis." It is also the basis for defining "church growth." But these theories have very weak understandings of culture—of the symbol systems, rituals and myths, belief systems and worldviews that shape a people's thinking. Consequently, they do not deal with the questions of cross-cultural communication, contextualization and theologizing in differ-

---

[4]Examples of this are North East India, Ruwanda and South India where large people movements have led to large churches, but where corruption, hostility and killing have continued, little affected by the gospel's power to transform not only lives but whole societies.

ent cultural settings. This explains, in part, the limited role that theology plays in church growth theory.

A fifth weakness is the problem of cultural relativism. British structural functionalism began with the much needed correction of viewing other cultures in Western terms. It ended in the 1950s with pragmatism and cultural relativism which reject all notions of social evil and cultural untruth. In missions this has led us to seek to preserve cultures at almost any cost, and to avoid judging the corporate sin found in all of them. In our Western churches, the spread of this attitude has cut at the central nerve of Christian missions. Many are no longer certain that Christ is the only way to salvation, and that those who reject him are lost. More see missions as cultural imperialism and see few ways to avoid it.

Finally, social missiology tends to have a weak view of history. It is concerned with synchronic models of social organization—with how societies are put together, how they function, and how they change. It has little awareness of the fact that cultures are always changing, and full of internal tensions and conflict.

## AMERICAN HISTORICISM (1910 - PRESENT)

A second theoretical challenge to the theory of cultural evolution emerged in North America, and came be known as American Historicism. It was pioneered by Franz Boas (1858-1942), A. L. Kroeber (1876-1960) and their disciples. They studied the North American Indians whose cultures had been scattered, and who were now living largely on reservations. For the American Historicists, the questions of change and the history of change were central. How had the Indians survived in the midst of such cultural turmoil? Why had some of them acculturated to the new ways introduced by Western settlers?

American Historicists rejected the arrogance and ethnocentrism associated with the word "civilization," and replaced it with the word "culture." This shift in terms reflects profound changes in how anthropologists began to view other peoples. McGrane writes:

> The emergence of the concept "culture" has made possible the democratization of differences. . . .

The twentieth-century concept of "culture" has rescued the non-European Other from the depths of the past and prehistory and reasserted him in the present; he is, once again contemporary with us. Twentieth-century "culture" was a concept forged in the teeth of "evolution," in a struggle to the death with "evolution" and the hierarchical scheme implicit in it (McGrane 1989:114).

The anthropologists used the plural form "cultures" not only to affirm their autonomy but also their diversity.

For American Historicists culture was not a bounded, tightly integrated whole. Rather, they described cultural cores and areas in the same way linguists were defining linguistic families and regions. Moreover, they saw culture as constantly changing, and change as potentially good. The American Historical school gave rise to a number of subdisciplines that have impacted missiology.

**Descriptive Linguistics**

The emergence of descriptive linguistics in anthropology to enable scholars to learn oral languages and to reduce them to writing has played a key role in the modern Bible translation movement in the last fifty years. The American Bible Society team led by Eugene Nida and including a number of outstanding linguists such as William Smalley, William Reyburn, and Jacob Loewen contributed greatly to the development of linguistics and to translation theory. They also pioneered the concept of dynamic-equivalence translations which are based on a diadic view of signs as made up of forms and meanings. Wycliffe Bible translators led by Kenneth Pike and including a long list of solid linguists such as Dan Shaw and Jon Aarenson have contributed much to our understanding of semantic analysis.

The positive contributions of these Bible translators cannot be overstated. Their fresh approach to reducing languages to writing, and to translate and publish more readable and understandable biblical texts has contributed greatly to the world church. They have also served as pioneer church planters in areas where no other missionaries are serving.

The introduction of dynamic-equivalence Bible translation has raised a number of questions. First, the use of a dyadic view of symbols as made up of form and meaning and the location of meaning in the heads of people renders the message totally subjective. There is no way to check such meaning against experiences of the external world and objective reality. Consequently, communication is receptor-oriented. While this is a good correction to the sender-oriented communication of the earlier formal translation theory, it removes any objective criteria for testing truth or for communicating it accurately.[5] We need to return to a modified reference theory of signs that affirms that we can speak about truth. It is here that the recent interest in Charles Peirce's theory of signs is helpful (1958). He points out the triadic nature of signs—the mental concept, the cultural symbol and the objective or external reality—to which that concept and symbol refer. Communication in Peircian terms is measured by the correspondence between what the speaker says and the hearer understands. This can be determined, in part, by both checking with the external realties to which they refer.[6]

Second, there is a danger of linguistic reductionism. Because communication is so central to human life, it is easy to use it as the model for understanding all human systems. This overlooks the social, economic, political and legal dimension of societies, and the complex relationships between social and cultural system. It also ignores the fact that communication is ultimately about something—namely events in history. In missions this can lead us to focus on the communication of the gospel, and to overlook the central question, "What is the gospel?"

---

[5]Wilhelm von Humboldt, one of the fathers of linguistics, differentiated between the "inner" and "outer" dimensions of symbols such as words. The former, he said, was the mental concept associated with a word, the latter its oral or written form. His student, Ferdinand de Saussure, labeled these as the "form" and the "meaning" of a word. Here "meaning" no longer is found in words that directly represent reality, but in the ideas and images in our heads. However, as Ludwig Wittgenstein points out, meanings are not private. Earlier Charles Pierce had noted that symbols are triadic and have an objective referent.

[6]For an example of such checking see Brent Berlin and Paul Kay's cross-cultural studies on color (1969).

## Acculturation Theory and Applied Anthropology

Some American Historicists focused their studies on culture change and culture collision.

They were interested in applying anthropology to social engineering and global development. After some rough beginnings, applied anthropologists today are widely used in government and nongovernment development agencies.

Christian applied anthropologists have contributed to mission programs involving development with agencies such as World Vision (Harley Schrech) and Mennonite Central Committee (Eloise Meneses). Missions have been slow in drawing on the insights provided by applied anthropology. The main danger here is to be pulled into a form of social engineering in which humans are in charge, and a social gospel that forgets the priority of sin and salvation. An example of this is the current interest in "meeting felt needs," and Maslow's hierarchy which puts spiritual needs at the end of a long list of human needs.[7]

### Ethnoscience

Following the lead of Malinowski, many anthropologists began in-depth field-based research in which they sought to "enter inside the head" of their informants (cf. Conklin 1955, Frake 1961) using linguistic rather than psychological models. The result was ethnoscience and componential analysis. Both seek to use the linguistic categories of their informants. Several subfields emerged including "ethnomusicology," "ethnobotany," "ethnopsychology" and so forth. The advantage over previous ethnographies is that the method can be precisely described so that studies can be replicated and verified.

---

[7]Maslow's hierarchy of human needs has been widely cited uncritically in evangelical circles. It assumes a linear progression—from felt need for food, to shelter, psychological well being, social belonging and finally spiritual meaning. If we follow this in missions, we will spend all our time on low level needs and never get to conversion. Moreover, it treats spiritual life as a desirable but not ultimately important need. We need to use a systems approach to human needs and recognize that immediate needs may be doors leading us to deal with the ultimate spiritual needs of people.

The new ethnologists have been relatively silent about the possibilities of cross-cultural comparisons. If each culture is described in its own terms, how can cultures be compared? Many ethnoscientists argue that valid comparison is impossible. One possible answer is to compare principles of cognition found in different cultures in order to find human universals, a tack taken by Claude Lévi-Strauss.

Ethnoscience has contributed to missiological thought through the work on ethnotheology by Chuck Kraft and on ethnomusicology by Roberta King. Others have applied the methods of ethnoscience to our emic understandings of cultures and worldviews. The strengths of the approach are a systematic methodology that allows replication of findings, and its ability to help us "enter into the heads of other peoples." Moreover, it enables us to get out, at least in part, from our own linguistic-cultural categories and penetrate deeply into the thinking of other peoples.

But ethnoscience has failed to remake anthropology. It is now one of the many streams in the discipline. In part, this failure is due to the fact that it has failed to provide us with a basis for cross-cultural comparison and for formulating generalizations. In the end, we are in danger of being locked up in different cultural prisons with no way out. Any attempts to develop meta-cultural grids for comparison are accused of being ethnocentric and a new imperialism. Lamin Sanneh accuses such accusers of being cultural believers and cultural prophets (1993).

Second, ethnoscientists tend to reduce everything to cognitive systems and communication. There is often a weak view of social systems and their power in shaping cultures and persons. There is also a neglect of history as the reality behind cultures, societies and persons.

Third, the cognitive model used in most ethnoscience treats knowledge as totally subjective, as existing only in the heads of people. As we have seen, this is based on the belief that symbols consist of forms and meanings. The result is receptor-oriented communication.

Fourth, in applying ethnoscience to missions there is a danger is letting the context determine the text of Scripture. Scripture then becomes what people believe it to be, not a communication from outside. Ultimately this leads us to an uncritical contextualization that is willing to bend the gospel to fit each culture, and to a neglect of its prophetic call for all cultures, societies and people to be transformed by the power of God. This subjectivism, rooted as it is in an instrumentalist epistemology (Hiebert 1995a:19-52), ultimately leaves us with total cognitive relativism and an inability to determine the truth. In this, ethnoscience is more a product of the instrumentalism of postmodern science that has emerged as a reaction to the positivism of modern science. However, like positivism, instrumentalism perpetuates the divorce of cognitive processes from morality and affective dimensions of human systems.

# CONTEMPORARY ANTHROPOLOGICAL THEORIES (1970-PRESENT)

For the most, part we in missions are about twenty years behind the current thinking in the social sciences. While we are still debating social and cultural systems, the growing edges of anthropology have moved on. Let me suggest a few areas that may have significance for us in missions.

### Symbolic Anthropology and Semeiotics

Some of the new insights into human realities have been the works of Clifford Geertz, Mary Douglas and Victor Turner. Geertz provides us with good models for fine-grained ethnographies built on "thick descriptions" that integrate social, cultural and personal analyses of particular human events, and, in so doing, help us to see them more wholistically and avoid reductionism.

Mary Douglas and Victor Turner lead us further into the study of signs, symbols and symbol systems, and show how these relate cognitive to social and personal systems. Here we begin to see the importance of sacred symbols and rituals in shaping and maintaining religious beliefs and communities. Given our Western rejection of formal symbols and rituals in our search for individual expression, many of us view symbols and rituals in other cultures as empty, dead formalism that needs to be destroyed in order for true inner Christian faith to find expression. But it is we who are impoverished without nondiscursive languages to speak of the transcendent. As Turner and Douglas show, it is difficult to construct and maintain sacred beliefs if these are not linked to the sacred community of the church and to sacred rites that give corporate expression to our faith. While retaining our emphasis on personal faith and piety, we need in the West to learn how to express our faith in the church using living sacred symbols and rites that renew and transform us individually and corporately. The awareness of the importance of rituals in religious life is particularly important in missions where we deal with societies for whom rituals are central to the people's lives.

Another new frontier in symbolic anthropology is the study of worldviews and their formative powers. We have often communicated the gospel in terms of surface behavior [don't drink alcohol, attend church regularly . . .] and conscious beliefs [Christ the incarnate son of God died for our sins. . . .]. Too often we have been unaware that beneath these forms and beliefs lie largely implicit worldviews that order the categories *we think with*, and the logic we use. Too often, we find young churches talk the right talk, but somehow we get the feeling that they are not saying the same thing—that prayer becomes a new form of magic, that the church becomes another arena for community infighting. There remains much to be done in the study of worldviews and in the definition of a biblical worldview.

**Religion**

Another new field in anthropology is the study of religions and religious movements. Tylor, Frazer and Morgan recognized the importance of religions as systems of belief, but discounted them as prelogical forms of thought. Social anthropologists have tended to follow Durkheim and seen religions as epiphenomenal—as the creations of societies to hold people together, and to enforce the community rules. They do not take religions seriously as *belief systems which the people are convinced are true statements of reality.*

Starting with Evans-Pritchard, some anthropologists have begun to take religious belief systems seriously, and to show that these are not prelogical or fantasies and projections of corporate minds. In recent years Robin Horton has done much to help us understand that the logic behind traditional religions is not some foreign logic, but rooted in human experience and in universal thought patterns common to us all. In so doing, he helps us take science off of its modern pedestal and to see it as one system of beliefs alongside other systems of belief.

Along another line of enquiry, A. F. C. Wallace (1958) has provided us with a preliminary framework for understanding religious movements. Building on his insights, Harold Turner has analyzed the impact of Christianity on primal religions and the emergence of New Emerging Religious Movements (1981). Much more study is needed, however, to help us understand the explosion of new and new-new religious movements around the world today, and the implications they have for Christian missions.

Taking religions seriously is an important step forward in anthropology, but so far no anthropologist has raised the next, and most vital question, which of these belief systems is true. All are afraid to move beyond phenomenology to ontology—to questions of what is really real—because they fear accusations of ethnocentrism and imperialism if they do. We can learn much from the recent studies of religion from a social science perspective, but they do not take spiritual matters seriously, and they fail to point us beyond phenomenology, leaving us by default in a relativistic morass. But as Peter Berger and others have pointed out, at some point we must confront the questions of truth and falsehood, righteousness and evil, or we are diletants and cretians who watch the world crumble and do nothing about it.

## A MODEL OF MISSIONS FOR THE 21ST CENTURY

Where does this leave us in missiology? Clearly we have learned much from the social sciences regarding the exegesis of human contexts, the communication of the gospel, the planting of churches, and the shaping of Christian worship, and there is more we can mine from social science theories. But we face a real danger. In recent years in evangelical missions, we have been so fascinated by the power of the social sciences that we are in danger of leaving our biblical foundations, and, in the process, of losing the heart and soul of mission. We need to return to the Scriptures to lay the foundations for a theology of mission for the next century (Köstenberger 1995). Let me suggest a few directions in which I believe we must move.

## Return to the Priority of Revelation, Theology and Mission

For all the contributions anthropology has made to missions, it can never be the foundation for missions. If we start with anthropology, we become anthropologists, not missionaries. We will never be driven by our social science insights to give our lives for others. We will reduce mission to what we can do for God by strategizing, management and effort. Only a personal experience of the gospel, a deep sense of God's call and the support of a community of believers will motivate us to go, and sustain us in the difficult times when we face loneliness, persecution, and even death. Only Scripture offers us a message of salvation for a lost world.

It is imperative at this juncture that we rebuild missiology on a biblical worldview. Like the early scientists, most of whom were Christians, we need to see the sciences, including anthropology, as branches of theology—as thinking the thoughts of God after him, not theology as the division of science having to do with God. In the latter view, spiritual realities are relegated to one discipline, and all the other sciences are totally secular. We must begin again with God and his divine revelation through his Word, his works and his Son.

We must also build missiology on theology—but not any theology.[8] Unfortunately, many who study theology in our schools do not hear the call to missions. They become pastors and professional theologians. Few departments of theology have missiology as an essential field in their discipline, or offer courses on the theology of mission. We must begin with a theology in which mission has a central place, if for no other reason than the fact that the Bible is essentially and centrally a book about mission. Neither missions nor theology will be revitalized in our day until they both are brought back together. Interestingly enough, when we begin as missionaries, we must be-

---

[8] We must remember that systematic theology as we now know it was born during the twelfth century as Europe rediscovered Aristotle's works which the crusaders brought back from Egypt and the Near East (Finger 1985:18-29). It was based on the same epistemological foundations as science, and many theologians such as A. Hodge, L. Schafer, W. Sheed and A. Strong defined theology as a kind of science. Like science, systematic theology takes a synchronic approach to truth and seeks for unchanging universals that underly all reality.

come both theologians who exegete scripture, and anthropologists who exegete human beings. As Martin Kähler said eight decades ago: Mission is "the mother of theology" (in Bosch 1991:16). Paul was the first Christian theologian precisely because he was the first Christian missionary, and it is intrinsically wrong to differentiate his mission and his theology (Dahl 1977:70). Paul's mission did not flow from his theology—his theology is a missionary theology (Hultgren 1985:145).

How can we bring theology and mission back together? Let me suggest three steps. The first is *phenomenology*—to carefully study the people in their contexts in order to understand them. Here anthropology can help us a great deal to see and grasp realities beyond our own cultural frames. One of our great weaknesses in missions in the past was that we often knew little of what was going on either in the local cultures or in the thoughts and lives of new believers.

The social sciences can help us understand humans, but they can also distort our vision by defining the categories, the logic and the theories we use to analyze human realities. We must constantly test these against Scripture. For example, the concept of "culture" as we now use it is a powerful tool in the study of people, but we are in danger of becoming culture believers. Like "mission" and "incarnation" the term is not found in Scripture. The closest terms in the New Testament are *archeon* and *sarks* which carry quite different meanings. Does this mean we must get rid of all these terms? No, but we must make certain that they fit with biblical teaching.

The social sciences stop with phenomenology, but we must move on to *ontology*—to judge our preliminary understandings in the light of Scripture. Here theology plays a central role, for it helps us understand truth and righteousness from God's perspective, and helps us communicate these to people in vastly different historical and cultural contexts.

The third step is *missiology*—leading people to faith and to the truth revealed in Scripture. We cannot simply condemn the existing beliefs and practices of new converts, and expect these to die. We must explicitly deal with old ways and lead the believers into Christian truth and maturity in one area of life after another.

These steps do not form a linear formula, rather they are part of an ongoing process of reflection and ministry in missions. We are challenged by our reading of Scripture, and by what we see around us. We apply these learnings to our ministry, but in the process we face new questions, see new things, evaluate them and apply our conclusions in our ministry. In missions, research and ministry must go together, each informing the other.

In this cycle of reflection and ministry, we need to bring feelings and morals back into the picture. The Enlightenment divorced scientific knowledge from both in an attempt to make knowledge objective, but in doing so it has reduced knowledge to correct information and led to a moral collapse. Scripture makes it clear, truth calls us to respond, and faith is not faith until we act upon what we believe.

Underlying this process of study and ministry must be the constant, careful study of Scripture on our knees, open to hearing it change our preconceived ideas; ongoing prayer that God will make his truth known to us through the Holy Spirit; and humble listening to and learning from our brothers and sisters in faith who can help us see the deep biases which we have hidden from ourselves. These brothers and sisters include those who have gone before us, those who are our associates, and the new church that God is planting where we serve.

## Develop A Full Orbed Frame for Understanding Humans

One of the main problems with the social sciences has been that each focuses on one or another aspect of human existence, and tends to reduce all explanations to this system of explanation. Psychologists tend to reduce everything to psychological dynamics, social scientists to social explanations and cultural anthropologists to symbol systems and culture. In missions we have tended to follow this lead and seen one or another aspect of human life as determinative of the others. In so doing we have suffered the weaknesses of reductionism.

In recent years there has been a move to see humans as part of several intersecting systems—or a system of systems. We can examine our species as psychological beings, as members in communities that are shaped by social dynamics, and as creators of cultures which shape the ways in which they see and live in the world. We need also to include the biophysical system of which we are a part. Above all, we need to add the spiritual or divine dimension to the model or we are in danger of a radical secularism (figure 1).

Second, we need to look at the way these systems affect each other. For example, living in known sin can lead to psychological stress and social problems. Similarly, social tensions can lead us to spiritual doubts. We are whole persons, and to reduce ourselves to one or another system of explanation leads us astray. This wholistic view also helps us understand the far-reaching consequences of sin which affects all these areas and leads to ideological bondage, social oppression and personal sin. This view also helps us see the greatness of our salvation in Christ which transforms all of these areas in our lives.

A full-orbed model requires that we include both synchronic and diachronic models of human existence. The social sciences have focused on the structure of human life, history on the story of human life. Too often in missions we have been either ahistorical, or astructural in our models. These are complementary, and we need both. Ultimately, Scripture roots reality and meaning in the larger story of God's works. If in our fascination with systems of human life we lose sight of the human story, we lose the central truths of the gospel.

**Formulate a Biblical Worldview**

It is increasingly clear that we cannot integrate the insights of the social sciences and theology until both of them are imbedded in the same biblical worldview. It is impossible to truly integrate a secular theory of humans with the biblical teaching that affirms their divine origin and image. We must base our theological and social theories on the assumptions, categories and logic of a biblical worldview.

I realize this is a controversial topic. Some will argue that there is no such thing as a biblical worldview. If not, then the gospel deals only with limited cultural and social matters at the surface level. It does not transform the core of a society, namely its worldview. Others will say that there are several worldviews in the Bible. This is true, but I believe that throughout the Old Testament God was not only preparing a people to be his witnesses (and only a few did so), but also a worldview in which the incarnation, death and resurrection of Christ could adequately be understood. For example, in the Old Testament, God began with the local word for gods, *el*, but he then transformed it, giving it new meaning through his revelations of himself to Abraham (*el shaddai, el elion,* etc.); through the sacrifices, festivals and temple rites; through Israel's history; and through the prophets—so that when Christ came, the Jewish concept of "God" was no longer pagan, but adequate to communicate the biblical message about God Jehovah. Similarly, the concepts of sin, sacrifice, forgiveness, reconciliation, mercy and love were shaped throughout the Old Testament in preparation for the coming of Christ who embodied them as fully as humans can comprehend.

## Reaffirm the Oneness of Humanity, and of the Church

Through anthropology we have learned much about cultural diversity around the world. As Lamin Sanneh points out (1993), however, we are in danger of becoming culture believers and culture prophets—making culture the supreme value to be preserved at all costs. But this leads us to emphasize human differences, to justify ethnic pride, and ultimately to sanction segregation and ethnic cleansing.

### One Humanity

As Christians we must look beneath the human differences that blind us from seeing all people as one humanity, equally created in the image of God. Parochialism kills the mission vision. The Scriptures lead us to a startling conclusion: *at the deepest level of our identity as humans, there are no others, there is only us.* On the surface we are males and females, blacks and whites, rich and poor, but beneath this we are one humanity.

Our oneness of humanity is declared in the creation account (Ge 1:26), and affirmed by the universalism implicit in the Old Testament (Ps 148:11-13, Isa 45:22, Mic 4:1-2). Bosch writes:

> The entire history of Israel unveils the continuation of God's involvement with the nations. The God of Israel is the Creator and Lord of the whole world. For this reason Israel can comprehend its own history only in continuity with the history of the nations, not as a separate history (1991:18).

The nations are waiting for Yahweh (Isa 51:5), his glory will be revealed to them all (Isa 40:5), his servant is a light to the Gentiles (Isa 49:6), and they will worship in God's temple in Jerusalem (Ps 96:9).

It is in Christ and the New Testament that the implications of our common humanity are fully worked out. We see this in Christ's teaching when he said, "You have heard that it was said, 'You shall love your neighbor and hate your enemy.' But I say to you, Love your enemies and pray for those who persecute you" (Mt 5:43-44 NRSV). War demands that we hate our enemies and brand them as Other. Jesus says, our enemies are Us, therefore we must love them and give them the good news of salvation which is open to all (Jn 3:16).

If we start with the view that at the deepest level some people are Other, then our attempts to build bridges of reconciliation between "us" and "them" will ultimately fail. Beneath all the bridges we build, we know that there is still the chasm of Otherness which will separate us when things go bad. If we begin with the fact of our one humanity, we can celebrate our differences because they are secondary. We must recognize the importance of "cultures" but realize that they do not constitute our ultimate identity.

In affirming the oneness of humanity, we do not deny the great difficulty in understanding people in other cultures. Far too often we claim to know what others are thinking and feeling, when, in fact, we are totally wrong. The more we study cultural differences the more we realize how difficult true cross-cultural communication really is. Learning to understand people in other cultures in a fallen world is a long and difficult process, but by listening, learning and living among them we can learn to know them not just as objects of our analysis, but as humans like ourselves. It is here that anthropology has much to offer us by its analysis of cultures and of cross-cultural communication.

*One Body of Christ*

In our mission to plant churches we must recognize that *in the church there are no others, there are only us—members of the body of Christ.* Peter's amazement at what was taking place can be detected in his words in the house of Cornelius, "Truly I perceive that God shows no partiality" (Ac 10:34)! Paul wrote,

"[Christ] tore down the wall we used to keep each other at a distance. . . . Then he started over. Instead of continuing with two groups of people separated by centuries of animosity and suspicion, he created a new kind of human being, a fresh start for everyone" (Eph 2:14-15, Peterson 1993:404). It should come as no surprise that in the churches Paul planted Jews, Greeks, barbarians, Thracians, Egyptians, and Romans were able to feel at home. This mutual acceptance of Jews and Gentiles in the church was itself a testimony to the world of the transforming power of the gospel. The unity of the church is not a product of the good news, it is an essential part of that gospel.

## The Church in the World

This raises a difficult question. How does our identity as Christians relate to our identity as humans? If, in mission, we come as "Christians" to "non-Christians," we are tempted to see ourselves as outsiders and superiors. If, for the sake of the gospel, we identify with people in our common humanity, we come in humility, as one sinner inviting another to the salvation offered us all by Christ. Bosch notes:

> We are not the "haves", the *beati possidentes*, standing over against spiritual "have nots", the *massa damnata*. We are all recipients of the same mercy, sharing in the same mystery (1991:484).

But the church is not only called to identify with the world, but also to be a prophetic counter-cultural community calling people into the Kingdom of God. Berkhof notes, "[T]he church can be missionary only if its being-in-the-world is, at the same time, a being-different-from-the-world" (Bosch 1991:386). This lies at the heart of mission. We cannot ignore the plight of our fellow humans, nor are we content to simply sit and commiserate with them in their miserable condition. We long to share the good news of salvation which was given to us, a salvation not based on who we are or what we have done, but on God. Therefore, we are compelled by the love of God, in every place and on every occasion, to invite everyone to join us in that salvation which God has prepared for all.

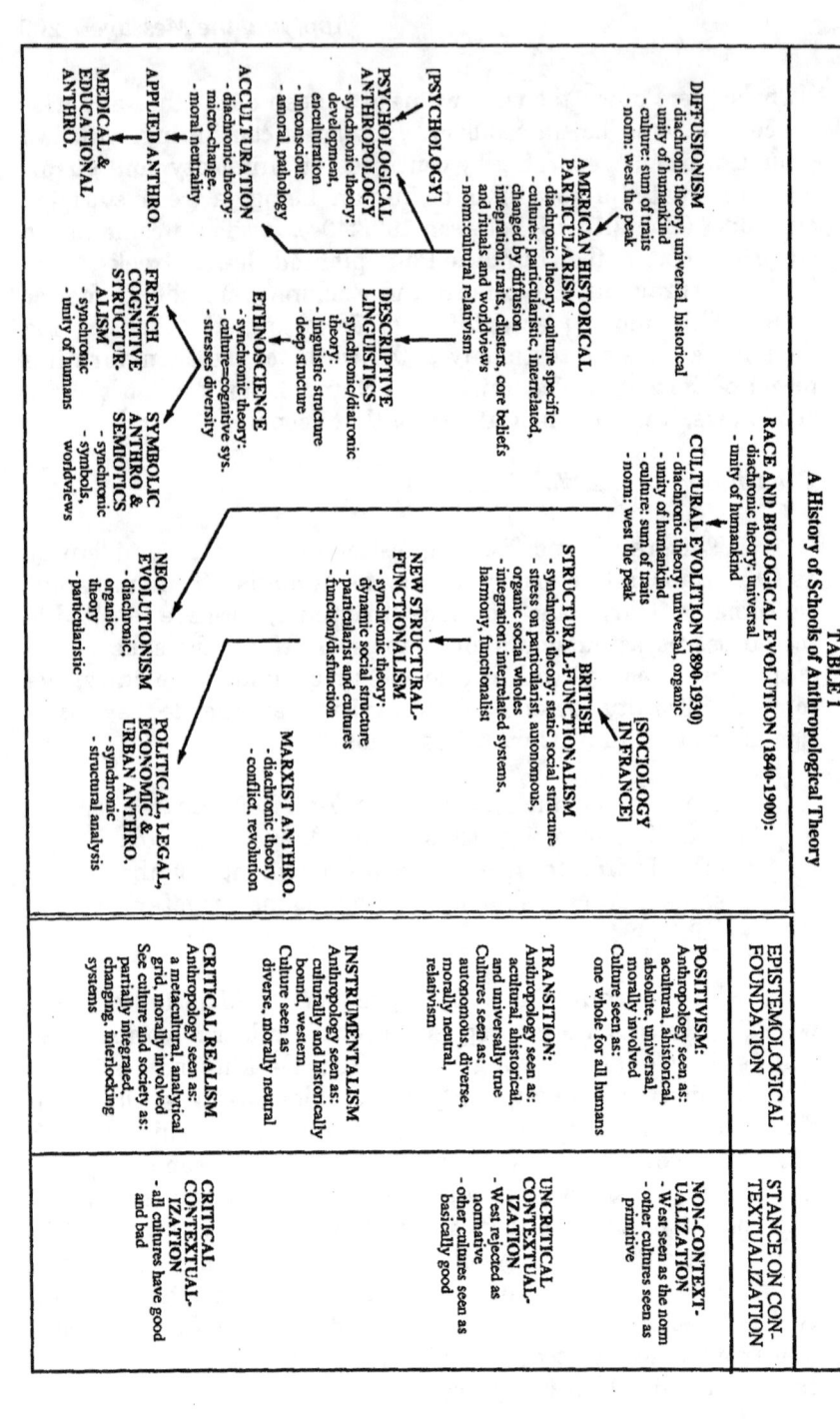

TABLE 1
A History of Schools of Anthropological Theory

# REFERENCE LIST

Anderson, Rufus

    1869    *Foreign Missions: Their Relations and Claims.* New York: Scribners.

Berlin, Brent and Paul Kay

    1969    *Basic Color Terms: Their Universality and Evolution.* Berkeley: University of California Press.

Bosch, David

    1991    *Transforming Mission: Paradigm Shifts in Theology of Mission.* Maryknoll, NY: Orbis Books.

Conklin, Harold C.

    1955    "Hamunóo Color Categories." *Southwestern Journal of Anthropology* 11: 339-44.

Conrad, Joseph

    1930 (1890) Heart of Darkness. New York: Signet.

Dahl, N. A.

    1977    "The Missionary Theology in the Epistle to the Romans." In *Studies in Paul: Theology for the Early Christian Mission.* Pp. 70-94. Minneapolis: Augsburg Publishing House.

Finger, Thomas

    1985    *Christian Theology: An Eschatological Approach.* Scottdale, PA: Herald Press.

Frake, Charles O.

    1961    "The Diagnosis of Disease Among the Subanun of Mindanao." *American Anthropologist.* 63: 113-32.

Hiebert, Paul G.

    1995a    "Are We Our Others' Keepers?" *Currents in Theology and Mission* 22(5): 325-337.

    1995b    *Anthropological Reflections on Missiological Issues.* Grand Rapids, MI: Baker Book House.

Horton, Robin

    1967    "African Traditional Thought and Western Science I and II." *Africa* 37: 50-155.

Hultgren, Arland J.

    1985    *Paul's Gospel and Mission.* Philadelphia: Fortress Press.

Köstenberger, Andreas

    1995    "The Challenge of a Systematized Biblical Theology of Mission: Missiological Insights From the Gospel of John." *Missiology* 23: 445-464.

Lumeah, Nzash

    1988    *Curse on Ham's Descendants: Its Missiological Impact on Zairian Mbala Mennonite Brethren.* Pasadena, CA: Ph.D. dissertation, Fuller Theological Seminary.

McGrane, Bernard

    1989    *Beyond Anthropology: Society and the Other.* New York: Columbia University Press.

Neill, Stephen

    1982    *A History of Christian Missions.* Harmondsworth, Middlesex, England: Penguin Books.

Newbigin, Leslie

    1966    *Honest Religion for Secular Man.* Philadelphia: Westminster.

Peirce, C. S.

    1958    *Charles S. Peirce: Selected Writings.* New York: Dover Publications.

Peterson, Eugene

    1993    *The Message: The New Testament in Contemporary English.* Colorado Springs, CO: Navpress.

Reining, Conrad C.

    1962    "A Lost Period of Applied Anthropology." *American Anthropologist* 64: 593-600.

Salamone, Frank

    1986    "Missionaries and Anthropologists: An Inquiry into the Ambivalent Relationship." *Missiology*. 14(1): 55-70.

Sanneh, Lamin

    1993    *Encountering the West: Christianity and the Global Cultural Process*. Maryknoll, NY: Orbis Books.

Shenk, Wilbert

    1980    "The Changing Role of the Missionary: From 'Civilization to Contextualization.' In *Missions, Evangelism and Church Growth*. edited by C. Norman Kraus. Pp. 33-58. Scottdale, PA: Herald Press

    1983    *Henry Venn—Missionary Statesman*. Maryknoll, NY: Orbis Books.

Taber, Charles, R.

    1991    *The World is Too Much With Us: "Culture" in Modern Protestant Missions*. Macon, GA: Mercer University Press.

Turner, Harold

    1981    "Religious Movements in Primal (or Tribal) Societies." *Mission Focus* 9(3): 45-54.

Wallace, A. F. C.

    1958    "Revitalization Movements." *American Anthropologist* 58: 264-281.

# PART III

# CONCLUSIONS

# 11

# CONCLUSION

### Edward Rommen[1]

Throughout this book our authors have explored the relationship between the social sciences and missiology. In doing so, they have mapped the benefits as well as the potential hazards of the missiological use of the social sciences. All of this is based on the assumption that the study of missions (missiology) is a theologically-informed discipline of sufficiently scientific character as to allow cross-disciplinary interface.

According to the Oxford Dictionary of English a discipline is "a branch of instruction of education; a department of learning or knowledge; a science or art in its educational aspect" (*Oxford Dictionary*, 416). This usage is based on the term's development as an antithesis to the idea of "doctrine."[2] A doctrine or an abstract theory is the possession of a teacher. The activity of imparting that material to students is what characterizes a discipline. This implies that a discipline should have a special "doctrine" or set of theories, including a base of support-

---

[1] Edward Rommen is professor of missions at Columbia International University.

[2] "Discipline, as pertaining to the disciple or scholar is antithetical to doctrine, the property of the doctor or teacher; hence, in the history of the words, doctrine is more concerned with abstract theory and discipline with practice or exercise." *Oxford Dictionary of English*, Vol. III, 415.

ing literature; a cadre of experts, trained in and able to impart those theories; a limited or clearly defined scope, i.e., field of study; and a clear definition of its relationship to the area of knowledge of which it is a branch.

In the matter of a discipline's need to possess a set of abstract theories, missiology developed as a response to a more or less spontaneous but officially eschewed activity. As a result, it can hardly have been expected to enter the academy with a set of theories. What it brought was a mandate to action, and theoretical constructs have often been afterthoughts in missiology. Nevertheless, theories have been formulated.

As for a pool of experts; many of missiology's achievements have been the result of interdisciplinary efforts. Individual contributions have been made by scholars many of whom, although members of the missiological community, were trained in other fields of study and who made extensive use[3] of those disciplines.

With regard to the need for a clearly limited field of study, missiology's interests include such apparently diverse areas of study as cultural anthropology, non-Christian religions, exegesis, statistics, systematic theology, and audience analysis. This has led to a sometimes confusing plethora of sub-disciplines, a seemingly unmanageable proliferation of domains.[4]

This wide-ranging interest grows out of the very definition of missions and the resulting framework of missiology. Missions can be defined as a function of the church which involves 1) the sending of delegates in order to proclaim the gospel to the non-Christian world, 2) making disciples, which includes bringing people to the point of conversion, teaching them all that Christ had commanded and establishing the church,

---

[3]This is not to say that one discipline may not make use of another. Consider the example given in the Supplement to the *Oxford Dictionary of English*, Vol I, p. 814, taken from *Lancet* 13 Jan 113/1 1962. "Sir Lenard Parsons ... had been the first to draw into the paediatrics of his time other disciplines such as biochemistry and immunology."

[4]See, for example, Alan Tippett, *Introduction to Missiology* (Pasadena, CA: William Carey Library, 1987), xxv.

and 3) focusing these efforts on all nations, i.e., ethnic groupings, of the world.

Missiology is best defined as the study of all aspects of missions. Given the definition of missions, this study naturally falls into four areas: 1) the survey of missions, which is a description of the current state of the church's mission on the basis of reliable verifiable information; 2) the history of missions, which analyzes missionary activity in the past by asking how and under what conditions Christianity was spread; 3) theology of mission which is to provide a delineation of the basis, the nature, the motive, and the resources of mission based on biblical as well as anthropological material; 4) theory of mission strategy involves an examination of the practical steps required for the fulfillment of the Great Commission, such as evangelism and church planting. This has to do with the application of the theology of mission.

Each one of these four subdivisions is a legitimate discipline in its own right. This can be seen from the fact that a) they are rational (scientific) activities, b) they deal with phenomena which are demonstrably discipline specific, and c) they have established their own "internal" set of ground rules for dealing with said phenomena.[5]

As for the claim to scientific status, all four of missiology's subdivisions are executed using a specific methodology, and are formulated in terms of axiomatic summary statements which are evaluated in terms of generally accepted criteria (Scholtz: 5-83). In other words, they are carried out in a logically consistent and systematic way.

With regard to the specificity of the phenomena dealt with, missiology must admit to a great deal of overlap with other theological disciplines. However, missiological disciplines, although they presuppose and depend upon traditional theological disciplines, are in a position to make unique contributions. In that sense missiological disciplines may be viewed as being

---

[5]For example, the history of missions has had to develop its own means of verifying missionary prayer letters, a source of data that it is uniquely suited and required to deal with.

derived from what could be called parent disciplines (Pannenberg: 228-231).

In the area of church history, for example, missiology is particularly suited for the task of documenting the development of mission societies, providing biographies of missionaries, and analyzing the circumstances under which Christianity was introduced to various countries. In the realm of theology, missiology seeks to contribute on the basis of its special access to non-Christian religions and cross-cultural data. In each case the work done by the missiologist will have to be executed in a manner consistent with the norms of the parent discipline. The missiological disciplines function to facilitate the flow of data at the confluence of traditional theological activity and the "real time" execution of the church's missionary mandate.

What then of the disciplinary nature of missiology taken as a whole? From what has been said thus far, it should be obvious that, whereas the four subdivisions of missiology may rightly be considered disciplines, it is much more difficult to make that claim for missiology in general. The traditional idea of a discipline is based, in part, on a form of reductionism. That is, on the assumption that complex systems have to be broken down into their smallest component parts in order to make complex systems and subjects more manageable. In his book *The Fifth Discipline* Peter M. Senge suggests that this approach exacts an enormous price. He says:

> We can no longer see the consequences of our actions; we lose our intrinsic sense of connection to a larger whole. When we then try to 'see the big picture,' we try to reassemble the fragments in our minds, to list and organize all the pieces. But, as physicist David Bohm says, the task is futile—similar to trying to reassemble the fragments of a broken mirror to see a true reflection. Thus, after a while we give up trying to see the whole altogether (Senge: 3).

This tendency is quite apparent in missiology. Given the sheer vastness of human experiences it must deal with, it seems quite natural to subdivide it, i.e., to break it down into manageable packets. But one of the greatest weaknesses of this approach is that the resulting sub-disciplines tend to become isolated.

Thus, theology of mission could be developed in such a way as to have only limited impact on the execution of mission strategies. This will be true unless we find some way of coordinating or synthesizing the work being done by all sub-divisions. This appears to be the task of missiology. It is a meta-disciplinary activity which integrates, synthesizes, and defines the work of and the relationships between the four missiological disciplines, their respective parent disciplines, and whatever additional fields of study it chooses to make use of.[6]

Any field of study which meets the criteria for being called a discipline will, by definition, develop its own methodology and domain of study. That domain will be but one facet of human knowledge taken as a whole. In most cases the objects or fields of study separate the various disciplines into discreet domains with little or no overlap. In the case of missiology, however, a number of its concerns are also the objects of study in other disciplines. This raises the question of how it can be related to disciplines which share similar concerns, but not necessarily its presuppositions and methodologies.

For example, missiology is vitally interested in the nature of human beings including such things as basic needs, social structure, communication patterns, and systems of belief. These are also primary concerns in the social sciences. In relating one of its own sub-disciplines to a social science missiology will have to:

- Identify overlapping domains by asking which of the social sciences is asking the same kinds of questions, searching for similar data. Of course, it will also have to ask if those disciplines are driven by radically different presuppositions and/or methodologies, and the degree to which that affects their explanation of the data.

---

[6]This is somewhat analogous to what industry refers to as a "quality circle," a special working group which brings together experts from various departments in order to focus on joint or corporate concerns. These groups tend to sidestep the hierarchical structure and provide paths of communication and cross-fertilization which are generally not available to its members.

- Establish areas of complementarity by asking in what ways the social sciences provided information and insights which enhance or complement a biblically-informed evaluation of a given situation.
- Establish a modus for the exchange and use of information.
- Acknowledge the final authority of Scripture, to which missiology may appeal in the event of discrepancy.

Given these basic conditions, missiology can make beneficial use of the social sciences in at least the following ways:

- Missiology may use the social sciences to help answer questions not addressed by any of its sub-disciplines. For example, Scripture does not provide much information about the development and use of technology. Nevertheless, understanding this area is an essential element in the understanding of any culture.
- Missiology may make use of social science to facilitate/complement its understanding of shared objects of study. Scripture does not insist on specific research tools and/or methods. It does not recommend specific models of communication. Many of the social sciences have developed techniques which are not at odds with the teaching of the Bible and do provide practical means of gathering information important for understanding the human situation. However, it is precisely in the area of shared concerns that missiology must be most vigilant against uncritical acceptance of presuppositions at variance with Scripture. This is not to say that missiology must reject all data gathered by a social scientist with differing presuppositions. For example, an interpretation of religious phenomena which is completely functional, i.e., rejects *a priori* the supernatural, may not provide missiology with acceptable explanations, but may still prove to be an important source of data.

In short, while the social sciences have much to offer, missiology must always look to Scripture to resolve The discrepancies which invariably arise with respect to the legitimacy (appropriateness) of social scientific presuppositions and methodology, the interpretation of data gathered, and especially the overriding concern of missions—the proclamation of the gospel of our Lord Jesus Christ.

## REFERENCE LIST

Pannenberg, Wolfhardt

    1973   *Wissenschaftstheorie und Theologie.* Frankfurt: Suhrkamp Verlag.

Scholtz, H.

    1931   "Wie ist eine evangelische Theologie als Wissenschaft möglich?" *Zwischen den Zeiten* 9: 8-53.

Senge, Peter

    1990   *The Fifth Discipline.* New York: Doubleday.

Tippett, Alan

    1987   *Introduction to Missiology.* Pasadena, CA: William Carey Library.

# OTHER MISSION TEXTBOOKS FROM WILLIAM CAREY LIBRARY

For a complete catalog write:
William Carey Library
P. O. Box 40129
Pasadena, CA 91114

---

**CHURCH MULTIPLICATION GUIDE: Helping Churches to Reproduce Locally and Abroad,** by George Patterson and Richard Scoggins, 1993, 8 1/2 x 11 paperback, 128 pages
An action oriented, practical guide which provides an effective framework for raising up leaders and reproducing at every level--disciples, cell groups, and churches.

**CULTURE AND HUMAN VALUES: Christian Intervention in Anthropological Perspective,** by Jacob A. Leowen, 1975, paperback, 443 pages.
As an anthropologist, Dr. Loewen is particularly sensitive to the human and personal factors in personal and group behavior, and he is especially competent in describing some of the spiritual dimensions in the development of indigenous leadership.

**CRISIS AND HOPE IN LATIN AMERICA: An Evangelical Perspective (Revised Edition),** by Emilio Antonio Nunez C. and William David Taylor, 1996, paperback, 544 pages.
Nunez and Taylor expand their earlier work on Latin America. This revision incorporates an insightful essay by Peruvian missiologist Samuel Escobar, an updated section by Nunez and Taylor, and an expanded annotated bibliography.

**HOME GROWN LEADERS,** by Edgar J. Elliston, 1992, paperback, 182 pages.
Provides an approach for the development of Christian leaders whether they be small group leaders, supervisors of multiple small groups or pastors.

**MEDIA IN CHURCH AND MISSION: Communicating the Gospel,** by Viggo Sogaard, 1993, paperback, 304 pages.
A readable and practical synthesis of what has been learned through the new wave of thinking about communications.

**MESSAGE AND MISSION: The Communication of the Christian Faith (Revised)**, by Eugene A. Nida, 1990, paperback, 300 pages.
Sharing the Christian life and truth is far more than using words and forms congenial to us, but strange and perhaps threatening in another culture. This book not only points the way to true communication but is foundational in this field.

**ON BEING A MISSIONARY**, by Thomas Hale, 1995, paperback, 428 pages.
A book written for everyone who has an interest in missions, from the praying and giving supporter back home to the missionary on the field or about to be.

**PERSPECTIVES ON THE WORLD CHRISTIAN MOVEMENT: A Reader (Revised Edition)**, Ralph D. Winter and Steven C. Hawthorne, editors, 1992, paperback, 944 pages.
This text was designed to be the missionary platform of essential knowledge for all serious Christians who have only a secular education. Used as a basis for mission courses for fifteen years.

**A PEOPLE FOR HIS NAME: A Church-Based Missions Strategy** by Paul A. Beals, 1994, paperback, 260 pages.
A masterful overview of the roles of local churches, mission boards, missionaries and theological schools in the biblical fulfillment of the Great Commission.

**PREPARING MISSIONARIES FOR INTERCULTURAL COMMUNICATION: A Bicultural Approach,** by Lyman Reed, 1985, paperback, 204 pages.
The purpose of this book (now in its third printing) is to enable cross-cultural missionaries to be more adequately prepared for the task of intelligent communication.

**ST. LUKE'S MISSIOLOGY: A Cross-Cultural Challenge**, by Harold Dollar, 1996, paperback, 198 pages.
An exemplary integrative study with missiological conclusions that are weighty because they are firmly anchored in careful, multi-dimensional biblical scholarship.

www.ingramcontent.com/pod-product-compliance
Lightning Source LLC
LaVergne TN
LVHW011817060526
838200LV00053B/3813